MW00934767

WHAT'S IN THE BOOK

- Color the cover
- Marine Biologist FAQ
- Fish anatomy
- ANATOMICAL terms
- Ocean Layers
- Fish form and function:
- body shape
- summer flounder
- Undulated moray
- Lionfish
- Rainbow Parrotfish
- AXOLOTL
- Favia moon coral
- Porcupine puffer fish
- Ocean shrimp
- Atlantic manta
- Clown frogfish
- Blob fish
- African tigerfish
- Sea Lamprey
- Atlantic blue crab
- Green sea anemone
- Pacific black dragon
- Common seal
- Atlantic salmon
- Giant isopod
- Japanese spider crab
- Open brain coral
- Piranha
- Bull kelp
- Green sea turtle
- Saltwater crocodile
- Copperhead butterflyfish
- Peanut worm
- Anglerfish
- MANDARINfish
- Whale shark
- Half moon betta fish
- Necklace starfish
- African lungfish
- Leafy seadragon
- Clownfish
- Stonefish
- Basking shark
- Cauliflower jellyfish
- Sailfin molly
- Sperm whale
- Giant plumose anemone
- Giant squid
- American lobster

SPUNKY
SCIENCE

A MARINE BIOLOGIST'S
COLORING BOOK

Spunky Science ©

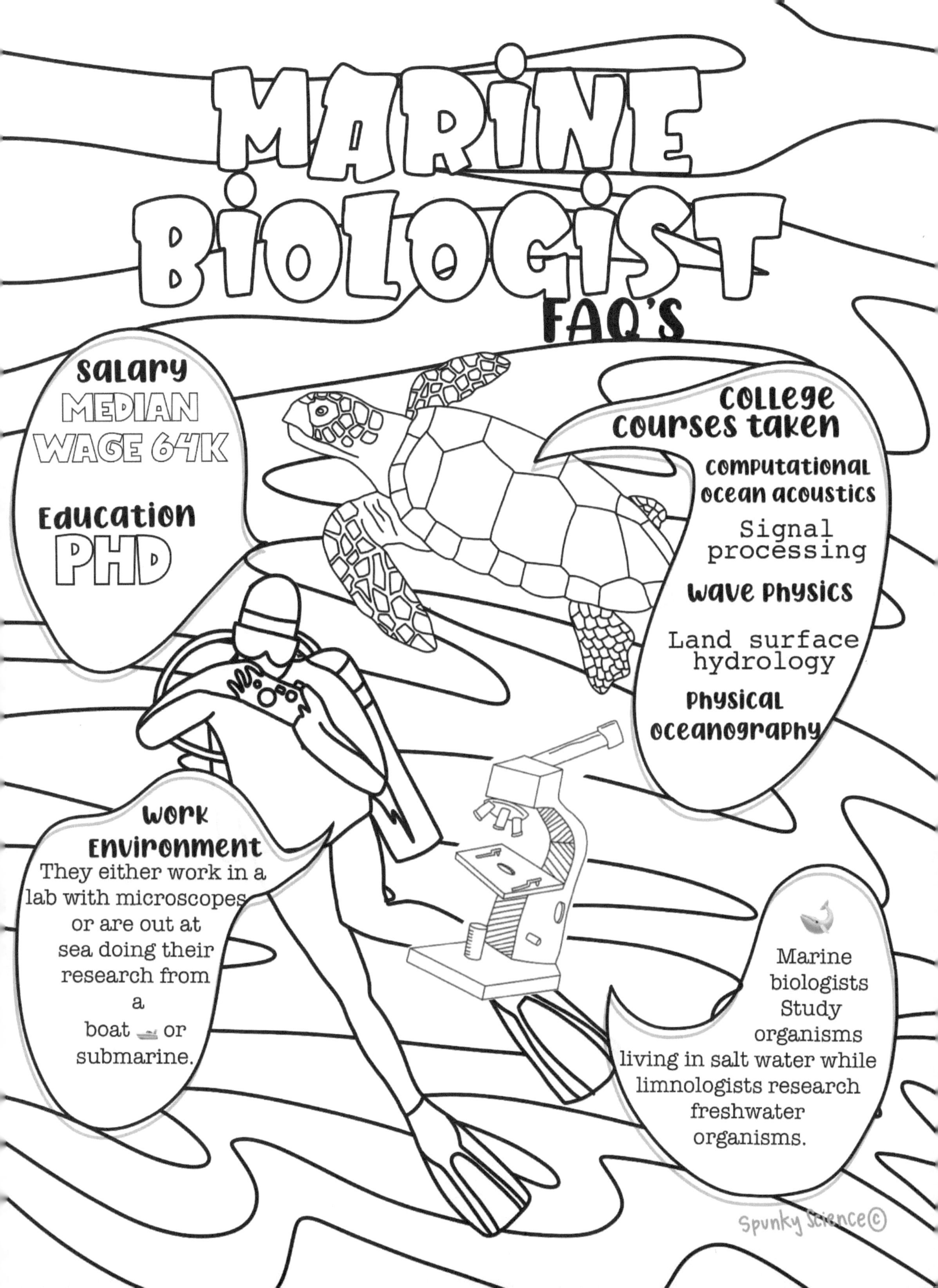
MARINE BIOLOGIST
FAQ'S
Salary
MEDIAN WAGE 64K
Education
PHD
College courses taken
computational ocean acoustics
Signal processing
wave physics
Land surface hydrology
Physical oceanography
Work Environment
They either work in a lab with microscopes or are out at sea doing their research from a boat or submarine.
Marine biologists Study organisms living in salt water while limnologists research freshwater organisms.
Spunky Science©

Fish Anatomy

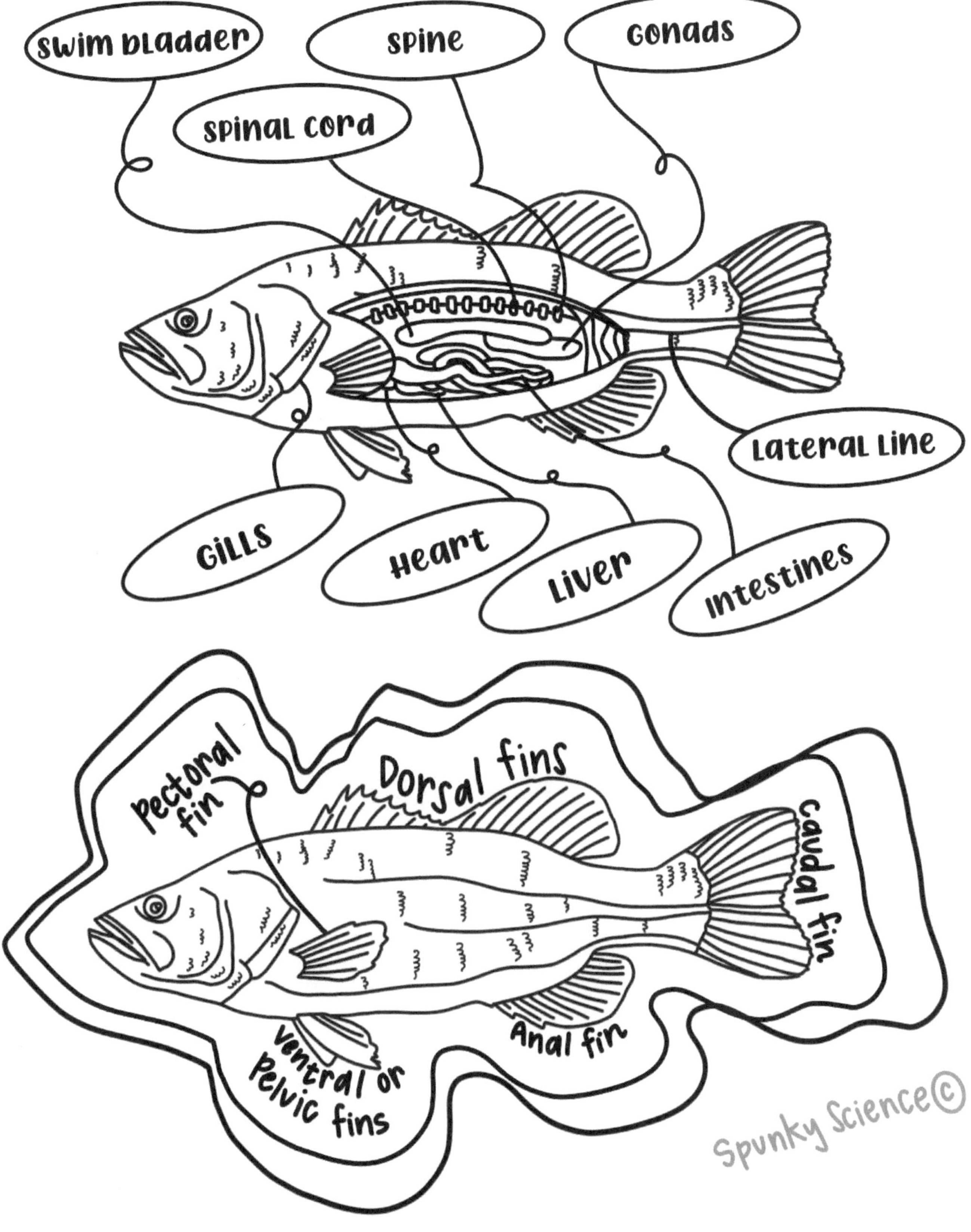

swim bladder
spine
gonads
spinal cord
lateral line
gills
heart
liver
intestines
pectoral fin
Dorsal fins
caudal fin
Anal fin
ventral or pelvic fins

Anatomical Terms

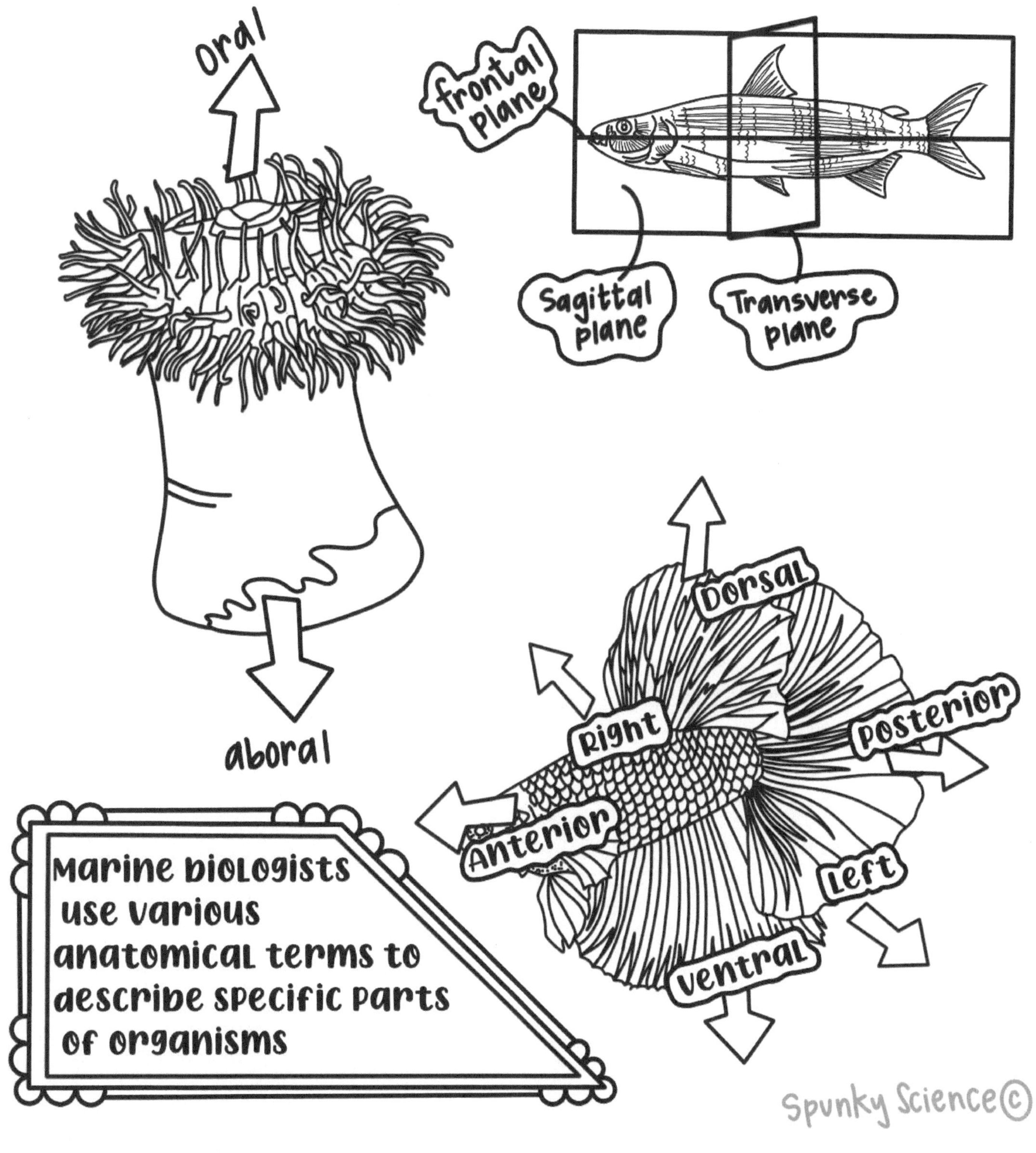

oral
aboral
frontal plane
Sagittal plane
Transverse plane
Dorsal
Right
Posterior
Anterior
Left
ventral

Marine biologists use various anatomical terms to describe specific parts of organisms

Ocean Layers

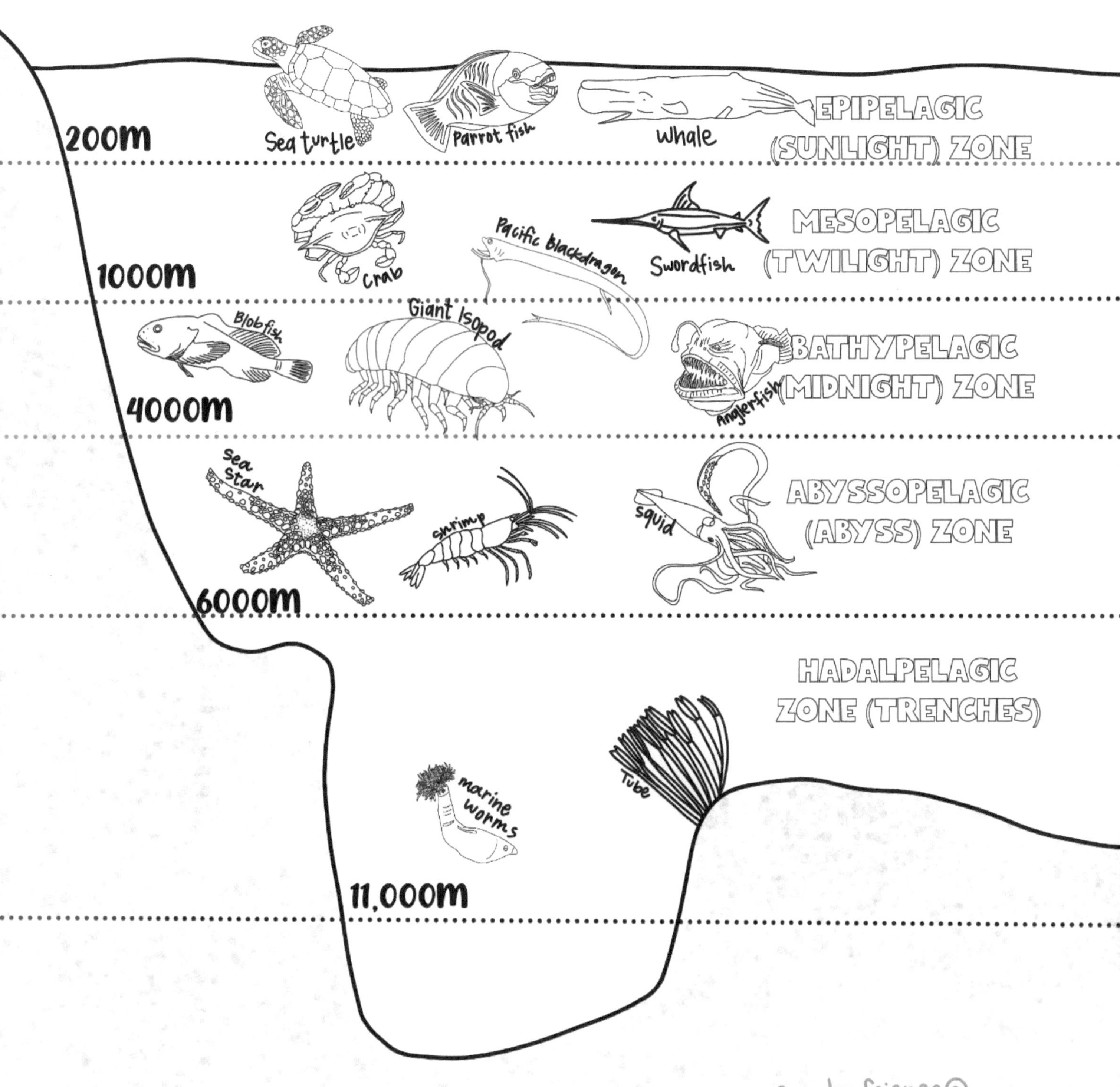

200m
1000m
4000m
6000m
11,000m
Sea turtle
Parrot fish
Whale
EPIPELAGIC (SUNLIGHT) ZONE
Crab
Pacific Blackdragon
Swordfish
MESOPELAGIC (TWILIGHT) ZONE
Blobfish
Giant Isopod
Anglerfish
BATHYPELAGIC (MIDNIGHT) ZONE
Sea Star
Shrimp
Squid
ABYSSOPELAGIC (ABYSS) ZONE
HADALPELAGIC ZONE (TRENCHES)
marine worms
Tube

Fish form and function: Body Shape

Body shape

Body type: Fusiform

Example
Tuna, salmon

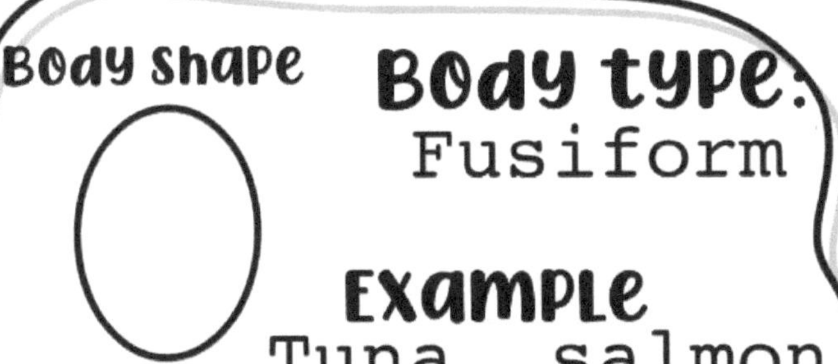
fast swimming. open water fish

Body shape

Body type: Globiform
Combination of shapes

Example
Frogfish, Lumpsuckers

may be slow-moving deep water dwellers

Body shape

Body type: Compressed

Example

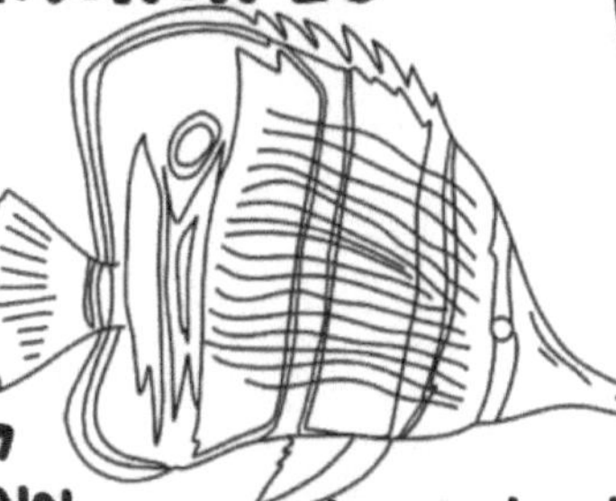
Not constantly swimming, bursts of energy.

Angel fish, filefish

Body shape

Body type: Depressed

flight like swimming, live on or near the bottom

Example
Skates, Rays, Angel Shark, and Flounder

Body shape

Example

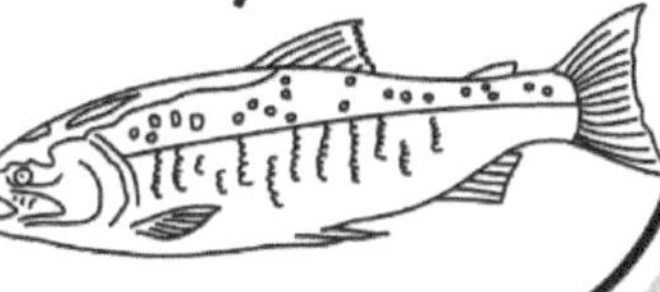
eel

long body. wavy or ribbon like, under rocks

Body type: Anguilliform
Eel-like

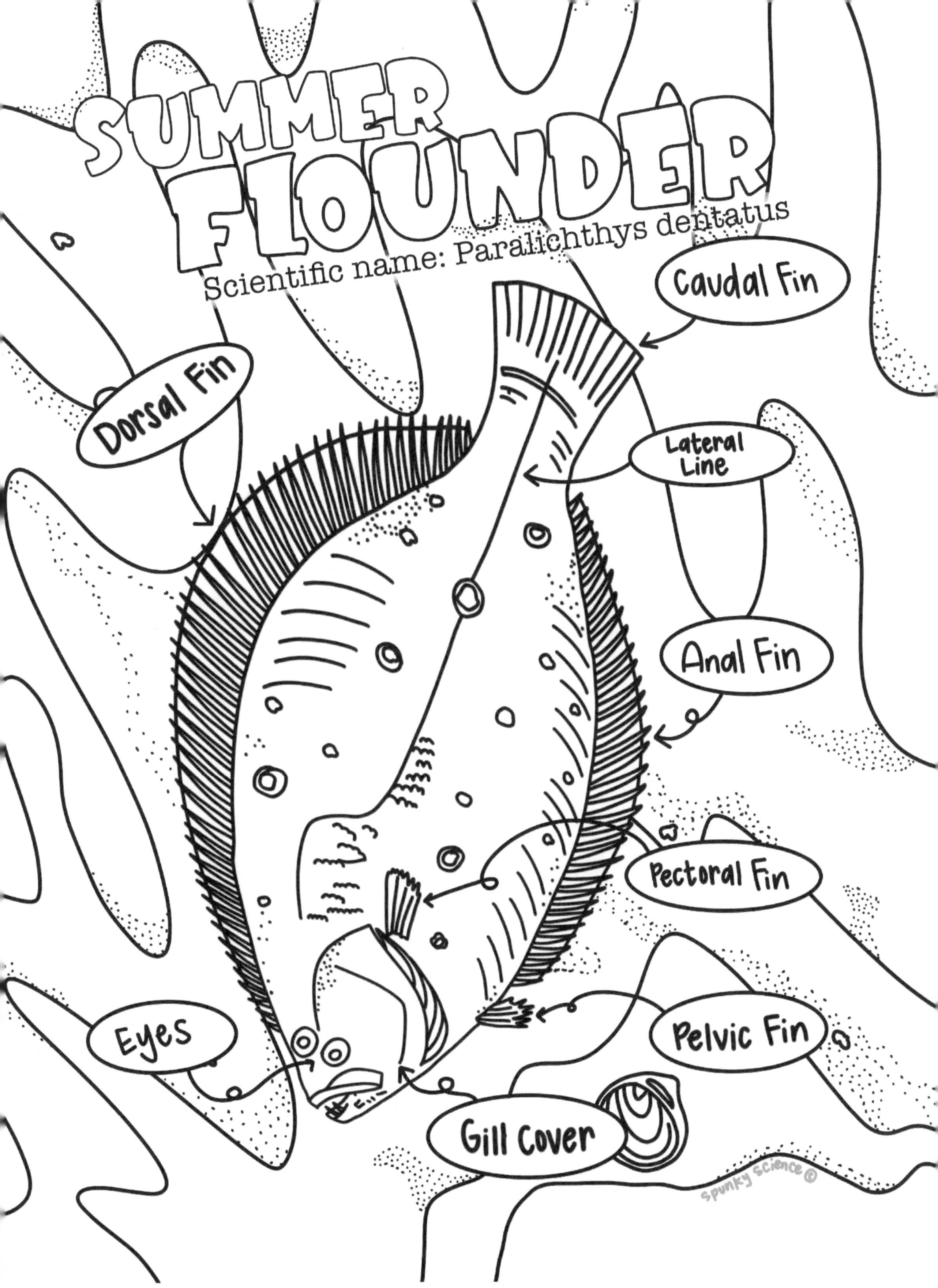
SUMMER FLOUNDER
Scientific name: Paralichthys dentatus
Caudal Fin
Dorsal Fin
Lateral Line
Anal Fin
Pectoral Fin
Pelvic Fin
Eyes
Gill Cover
spunky science ©

UNDULATED MORAY
scientific name: Gymnothorax undulatus
Eels emerge at night to hunt their prey which they locate with their strong sense of smell.
The mouth is held open so that water can be pumped over the gills.
Lacks fins to allow them to move within the narrow crevices of the reefs.
Spunky Science©

LIONFISH

Scientific name:
Pterosaurs volitans

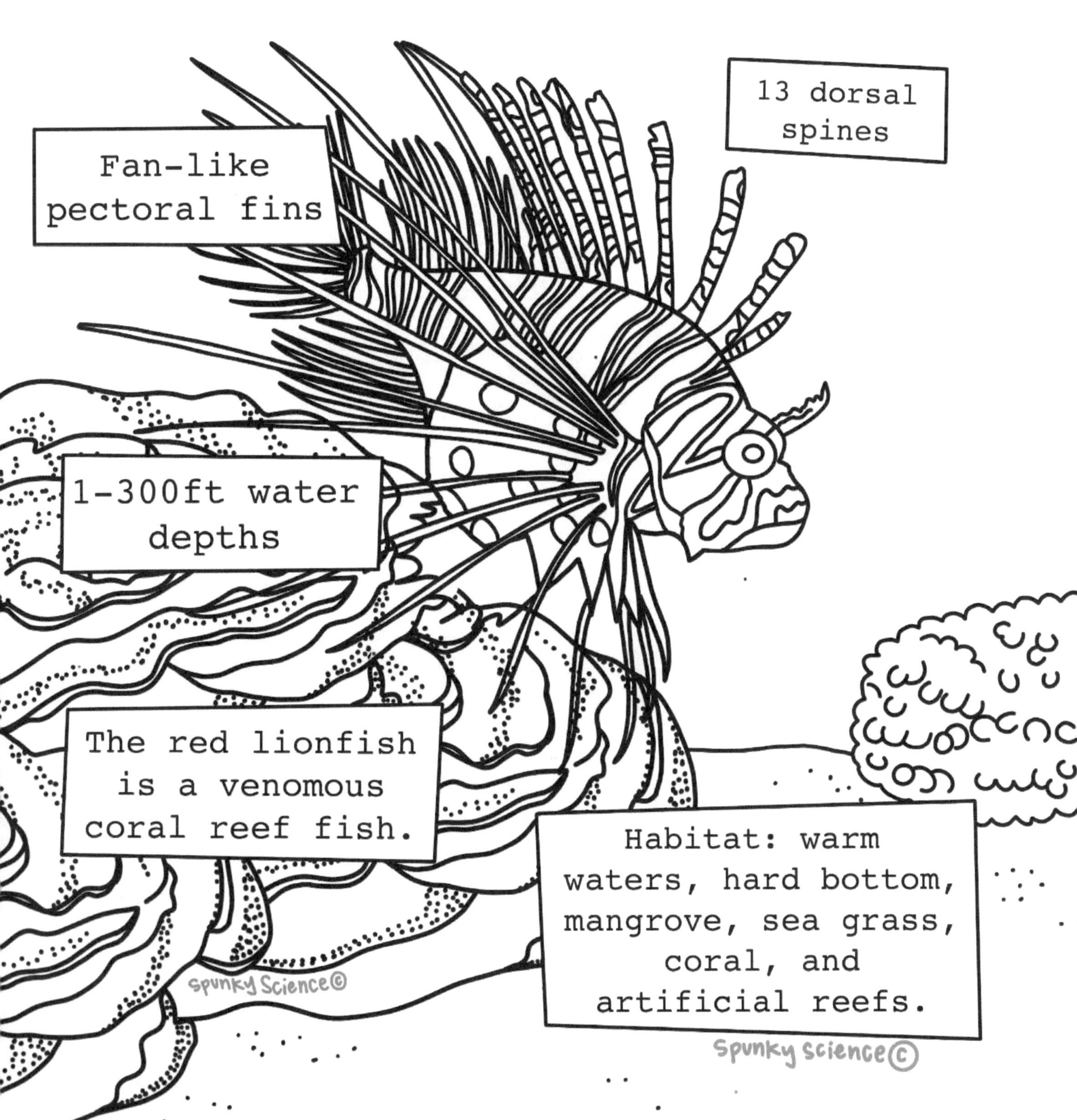

13 dorsal spines
Fan-like pectoral fins
1-300ft water depths
The red lionfish is a venomous coral reef fish.
Habitat: warm waters, hard bottom, mangrove, sea grass, coral, and artificial reefs.
Spunky Science©
Spunky Science©

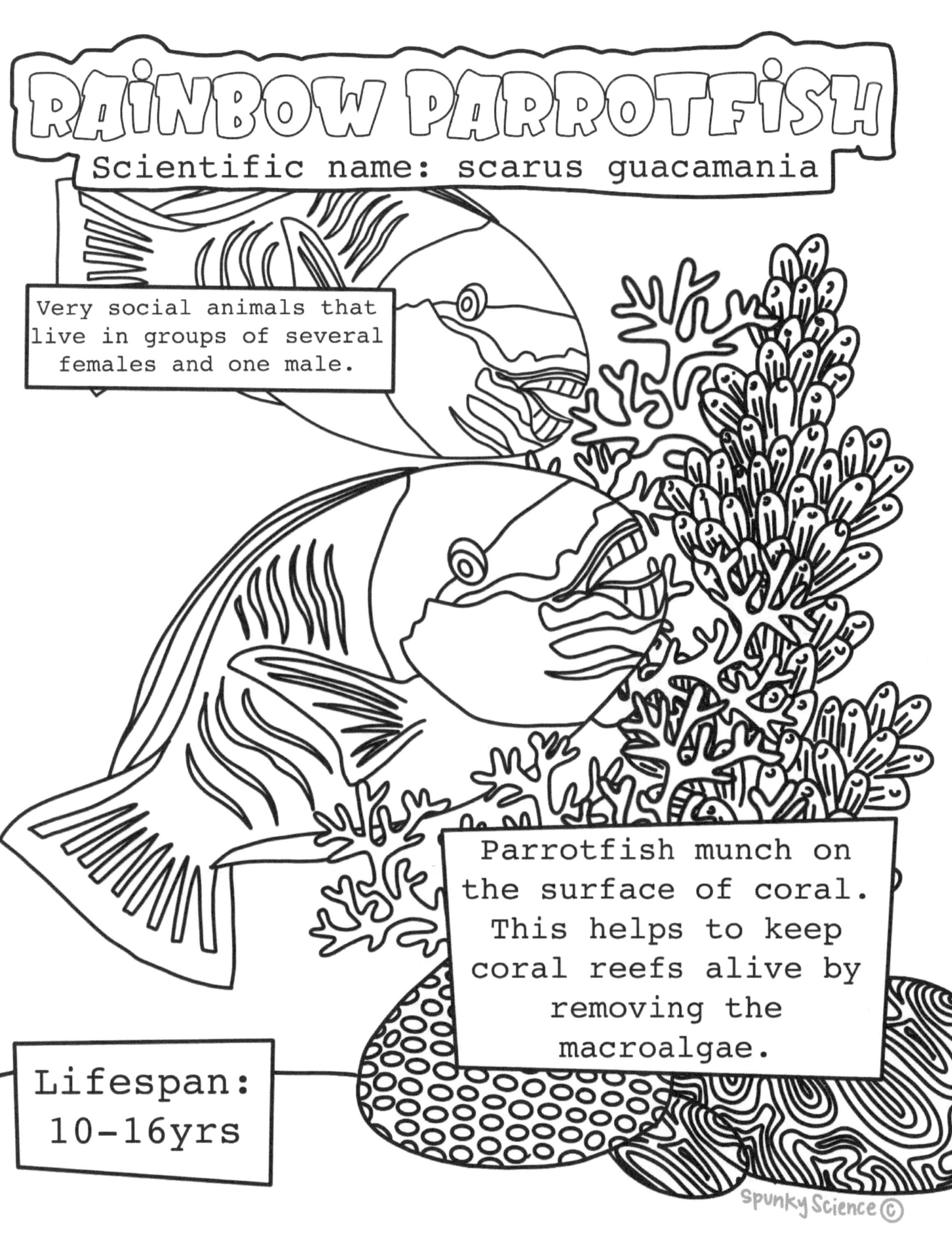
RAINBOW PARROTFISH
Scientific name: scarus guacamania
Very social animals that live in groups of several females and one male.
Parrotfish munch on the surface of coral. This helps to keep coral reefs alive by removing the macroalgae.
Lifespan: 10-16yrs
Spunky Science ©

AXOLOTL

Scientific name: Ambystoma mexicanum

Live up to
10 years
External gills
Coastal grooves
are used in
thermoregulation
and help to keep
the skin moist.
Diet: mollusks, worms,
insect larvae, crustaceans,
and some fish.
Axolotls have the ability
to completely
regenerate an entire
limb when lost!
Dorsal fin
Spunky Science ©

FAVIA MOON CORAL

Scientific name: Favia pallida

Common species to keep in an aquarium.

Favia corals can be aggressive because their sweeper tentacles can come out at night and sting other corals

Common names are Brain coral, Moon coral, Pineapple coral, Closed brain coral

Porcupine Puffer Fish

Scientific name:Diodon holocanthus

Defense: When agitated, pufferfish expand. Their organs contain a neurotoxin that is 1,200x more toxic than cyanide.
Excellent vision for seeing predators.
Diet: eating mollusks and other invertebrates wears down their teeth.

Ocean
SHRIMP

Scientific name: Pandalus jordani

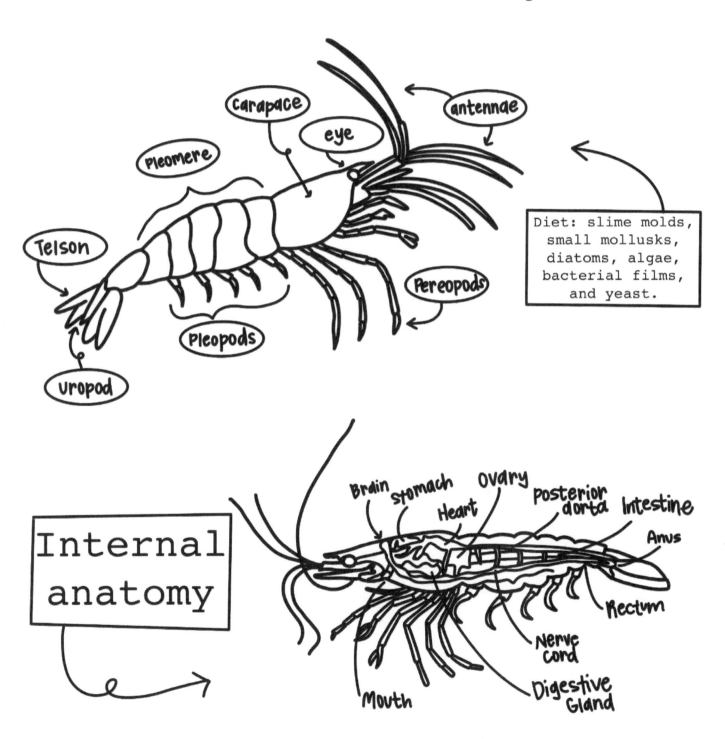

Carapace

eye

antennae

Pleomere

Telson

Pleopods

Pereopods

Uropod

Diet: slime molds, small mollusks, diatoms, algae, bacterial films, and yeast.

Internal anatomy

Brain

Stomach

Heart

Ovary

posterior aorta

Intestine

Anus

Rectum

Nerve cord

Digestive Gland

Mouth

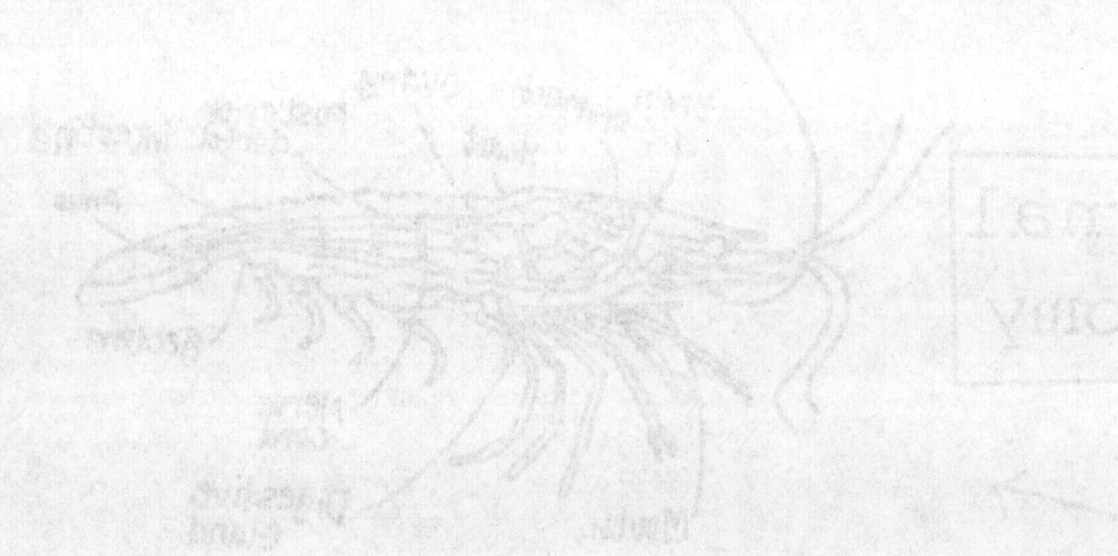

ATLANTIC MANTA

SCIENTIFIC NAME: MANTA BIROS

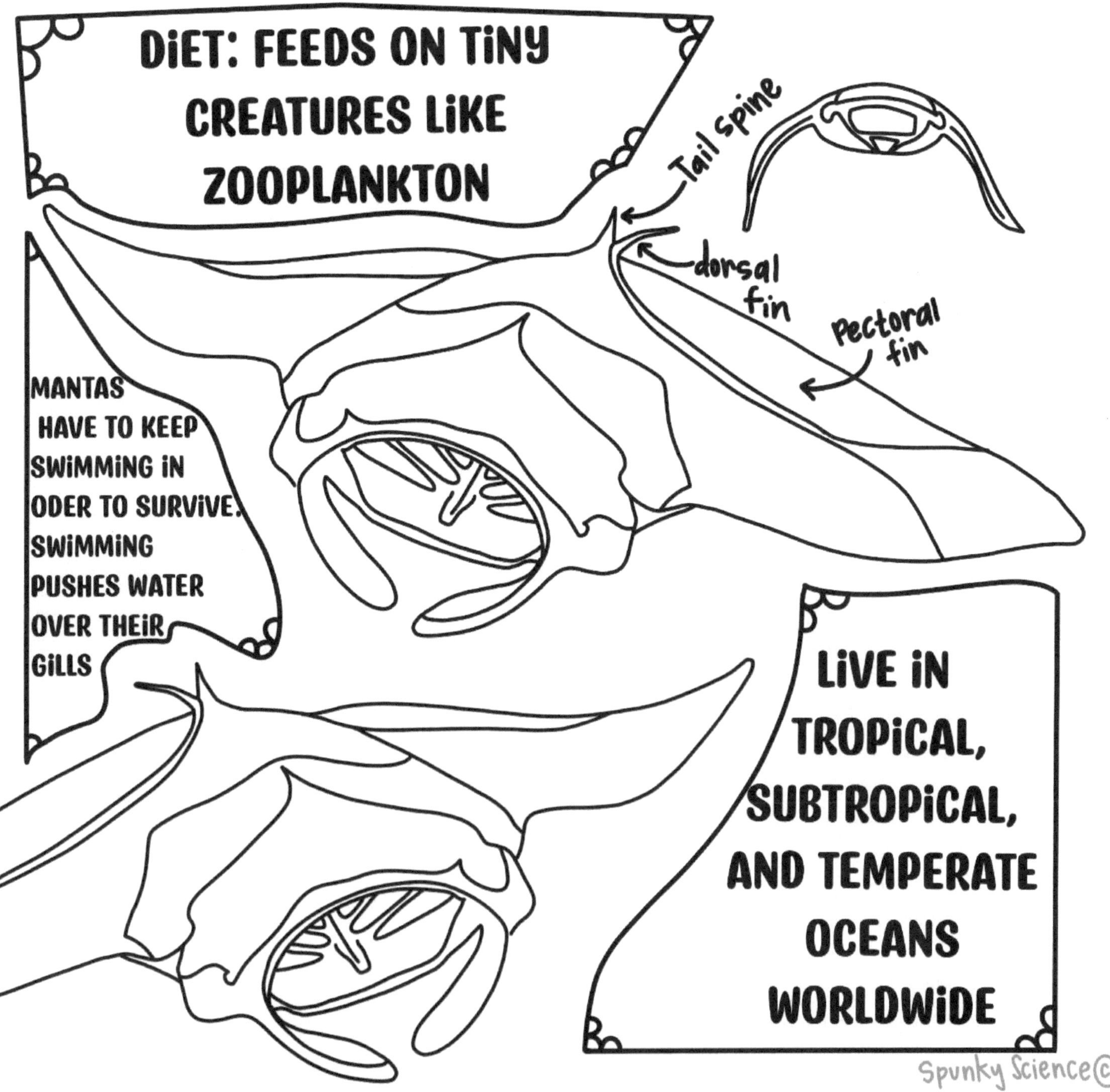

DIET: FEEDS ON TINY CREATURES LIKE ZOOPLANKTON
Tail spine
dorsal fin
Pectoral fin
MANTAS HAVE TO KEEP SWIMMING IN ODER TO SURVIVE. SWIMMING PUSHES WATER OVER THEIR GILLS
LIVE IN TROPICAL, SUBTROPICAL, AND TEMPERATE OCEANS WORLDWIDE

CLOWN
FROGFISH
Scientific name: Antennarius maculatus

During one mating period, a single Frogfish can lay between 40,000 to 180,000 eggs to be fertilized.

Flexible mouth and jaw allows frogfish to eat prey up to twice their size.

Frogfish are a type of anglerfish. This means that they have a protrusion on their heads that acts as a bait to other fish.

Frogfish is not born with a swim bladder. Instead of swimming, they use their fins to move around the bottom of the water.

BLOB FISH

Scientific name:
Psychrolutes marcidus

Above the surface

Lack a swim bladder

Diet: They do not hunt, they wait patiently for their food to come and then they consume it. Diet includes slugs, sea urchins, and snails.

Blobfish look like normal fish at their normal depths of 2,000-4,000 feet under the surface.

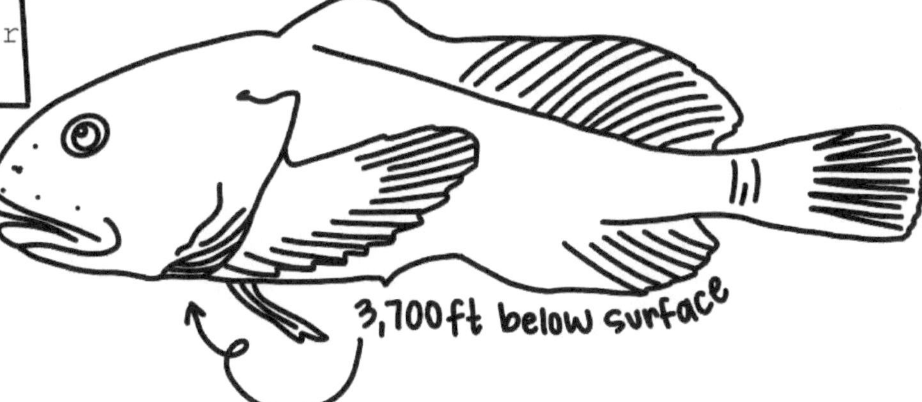
3,700ft below surface

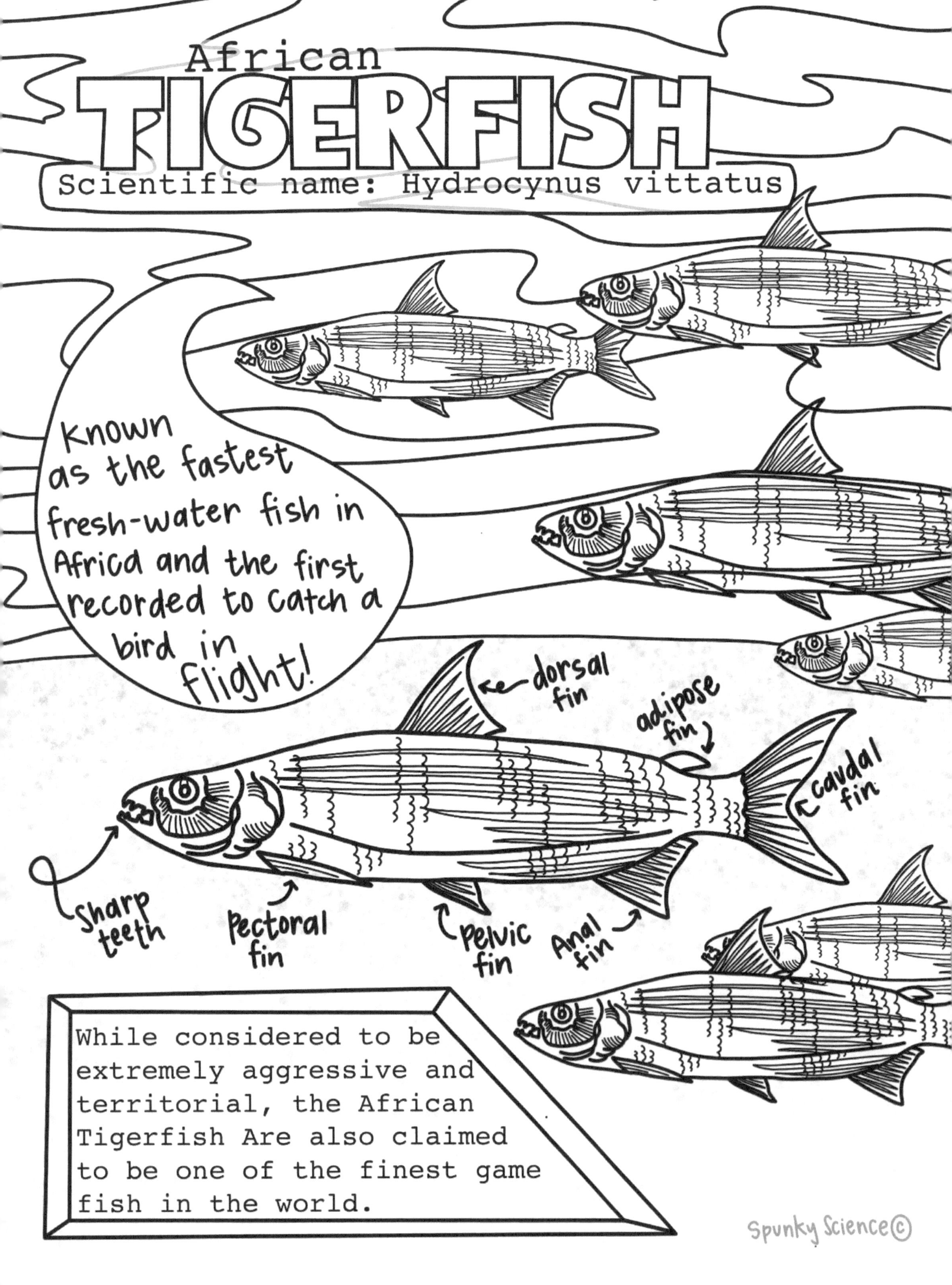
African
TIGERFISH
Scientific name: Hydrocynus vittatus
Known as the fastest fresh-water fish in Africa and the first recorded to catch a bird in flight!
dorsal fin
adipose fin
caudal fin
sharp teeth
pectoral fin
pelvic fin
Anal fin
While considered to be extremely aggressive and territorial, the African Tigerfish Are also claimed to be one of the finest game fish in the world.
Spunky Science©

SEA LAMPREY

SCIENTIFIC NAME:PETROMYZON MARINUS

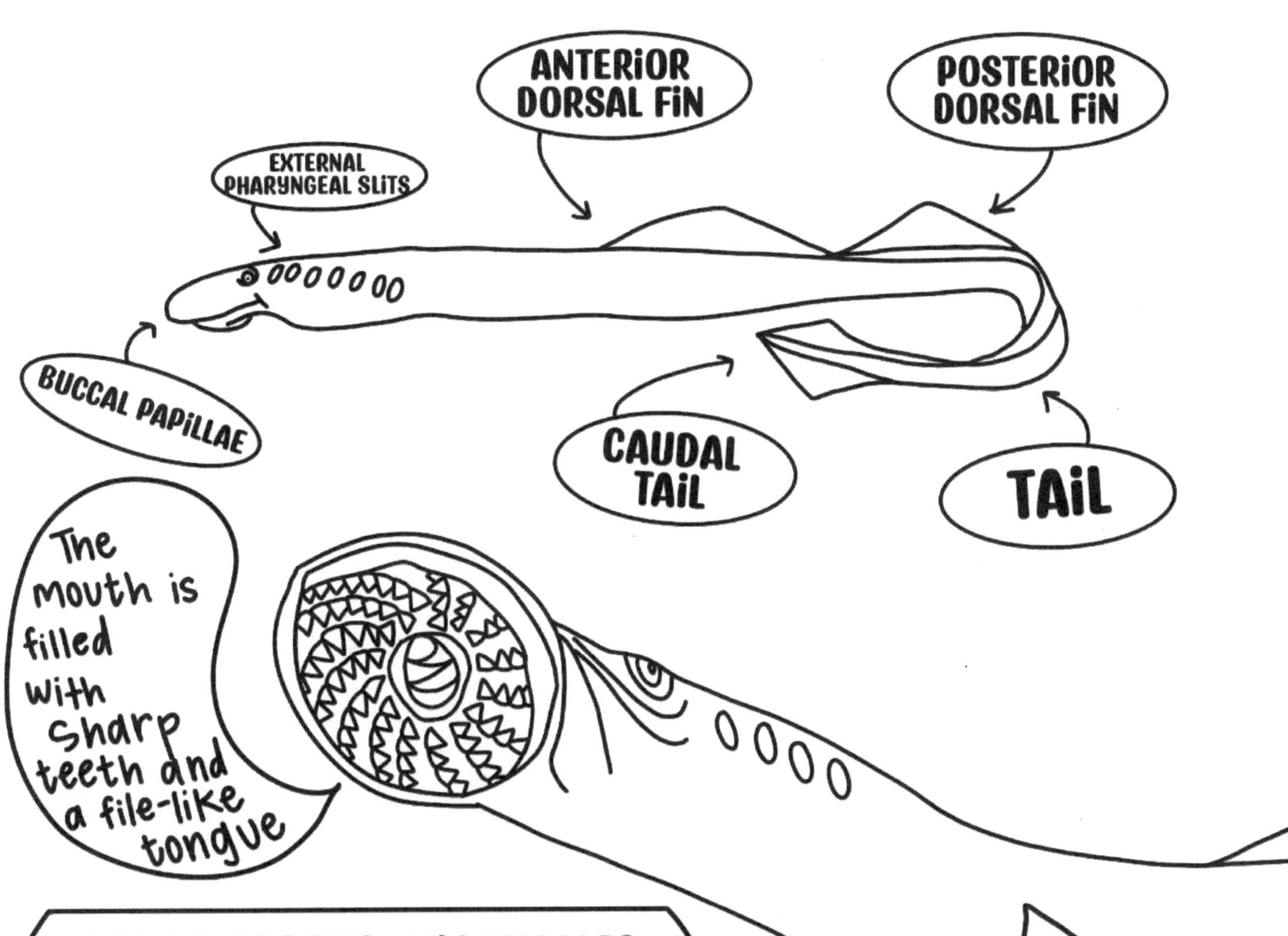

ANTERIOR DORSAL FIN
POSTERIOR DORSAL FIN
EXTERNAL PHARYNGEAL SLITS
BUCCAL PAPILLAE
CAUDAL TAIL
TAIL
The mouth is filled with sharp teeth and a file-like tongue
Sea lampreys are invasive and outcompete Great Lakes fish. Their invasion brought on the lake trout collapse

SEA LAMPREYS, NICKNAMED "VAMPIRE FISH" ARE PARASITIC FISH THAT PARASITIC EAT OTHER FISH BY SUCKING THEIR BLOOD AND OTHER BODY FLUIDS.

ATLANTIC BLUE CRAB

Scientific name: Callinectes sapidus

Average lifespan is 1-4 years in the wild
Blue crab got its name by its blue tinted claws.
Megalopa
Juvenile
zoea
eggs
LIFE CYCLE
Adult Female (eggs=sponge)
Adult
Diet: their main foods are small fish, snails, mussels, and plants. If there's nothing to eat, they'll eat other blue crabs too!

GREEN SEA ANEMONE

These anemones are carnivores, feeding on crabs, mussels, small fishes and sea urchins.
They cover their bodies with pieces of shell and gravel, which helps to reflect sunlight, hold in moisture and keep the animals cool when the tide drops.
Uses stinging cells found on its tentacles to paralyze its prey.
Spunky Science©

PACIFIC BLACKDRAGON

SCIENTIFIC NAME: IDACANTHUS ASTROSTOMUS

DIET: SMALL FISHES, SHRIMP, WORMS, CRABS, SQUID, AND BARNACLES.

THE MALES ARE MUCH SMALLER, HAVE NO TEETH, NO STOMACH OR BARBEL AND ARE UNABLE TO FEED.

STOMACHS ARE COATED WITH BLACK TISSUE TO BLOCK OUT LIGHT THAT MAY BE PRODUCED BY THE PREY THAT THEY HAVE EATEN.

A SEPARATE LIGHT ORGAN THAT IS USED TO ATTRACT PREY.

DEEP-SEA PREDATORS THAT LIVE IN THE DEEP WATERS OF THE EASTERN PACIFIC OCEAN/

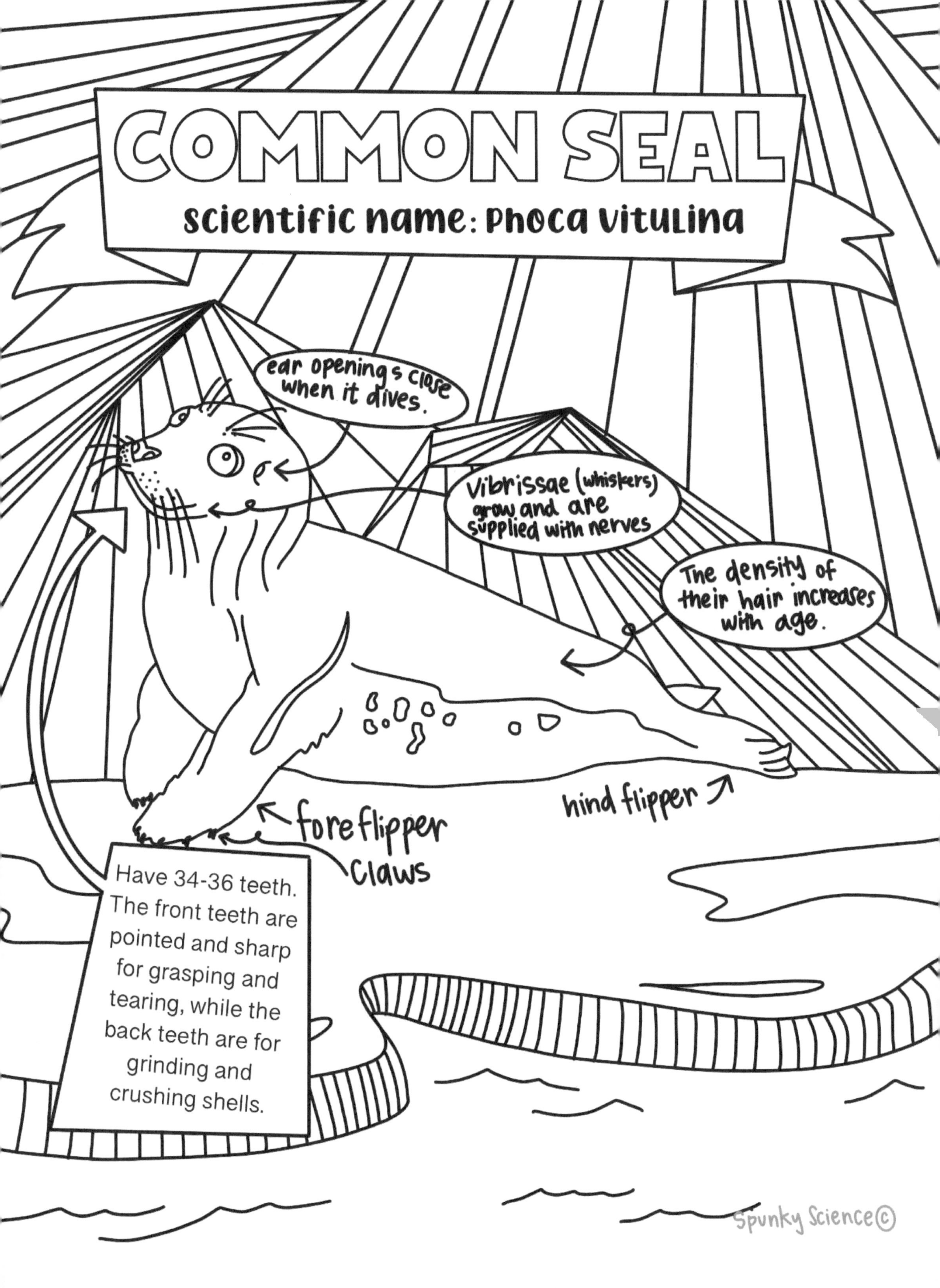
COMMON SEAL
scientific name: Phoca vitulina
ear openings close when it dives.
Vibrissae (whiskers) grow and are supplied with nerves
The density of their hair increases with age.
hind flipper
fore flipper
claws
Have 34-36 teeth. The front teeth are pointed and sharp for grasping and tearing, while the back teeth are for grinding and crushing shells.
Spunky Science©

atlantic
SALMON
Scientific name: Salmo salar

Atlantic Salmon are incredible in the way that they migrate thousands of miles during their lifetime

External Anatomy

1. Eyes
2. Dorsal fin
3. Adipose fin
4. Caudal fin
5. Lateral line
6. Anal fin
7. Pelvic fin
8. Pectoral fin
9. Gills and gill cover
10. Mouth

Live in both freshwater and saltwater habitats

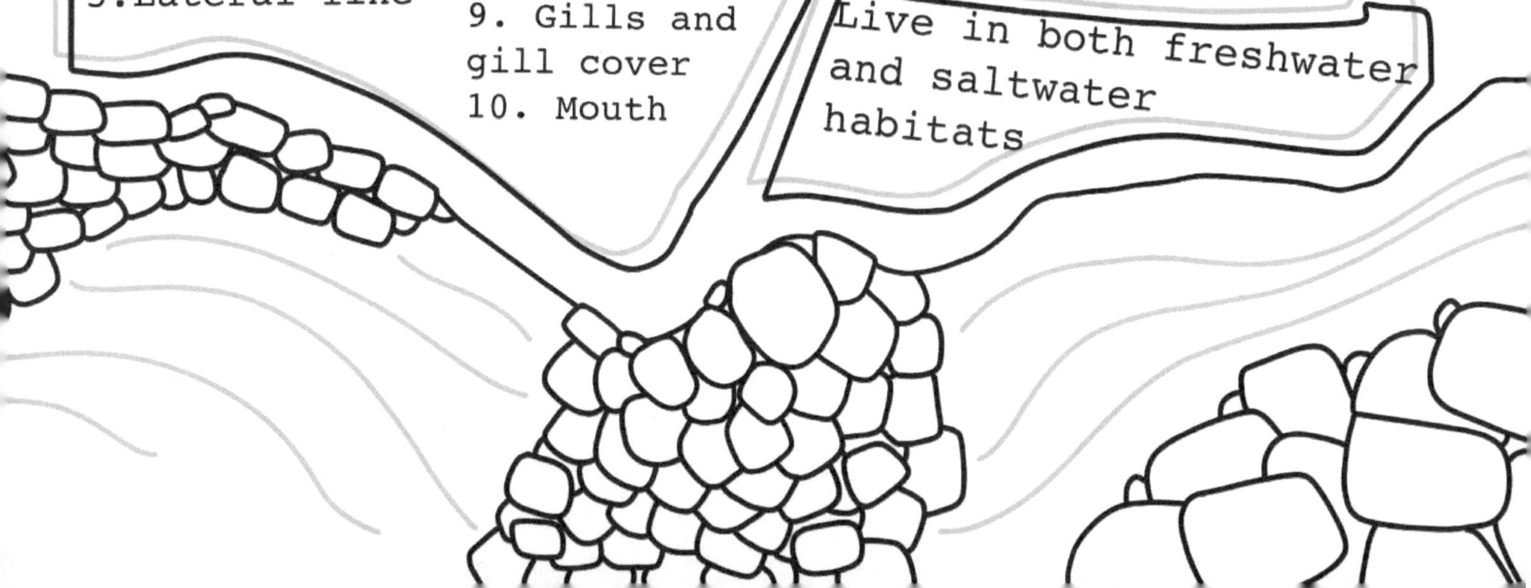

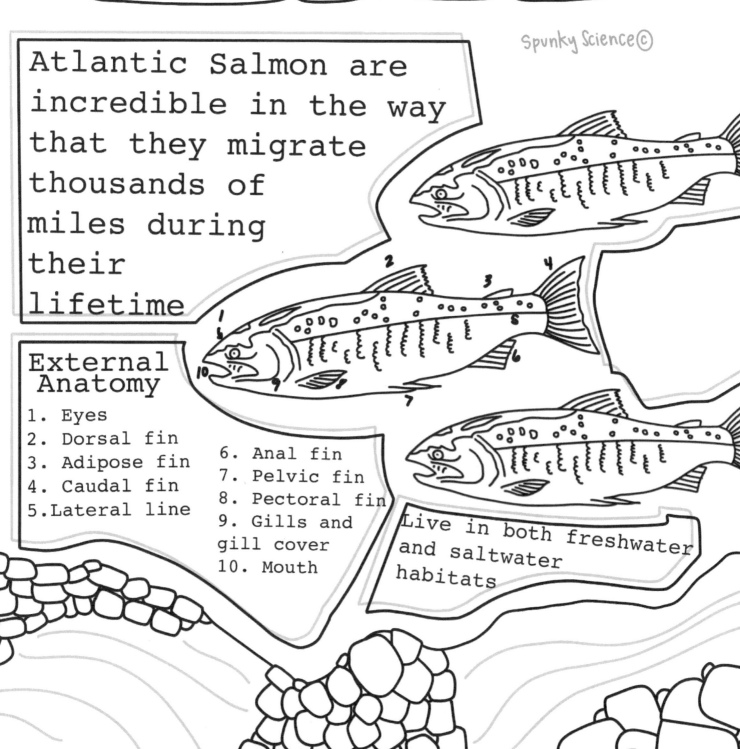

GIANT ISOPOD

Scientific name: Bathynomus giganteus

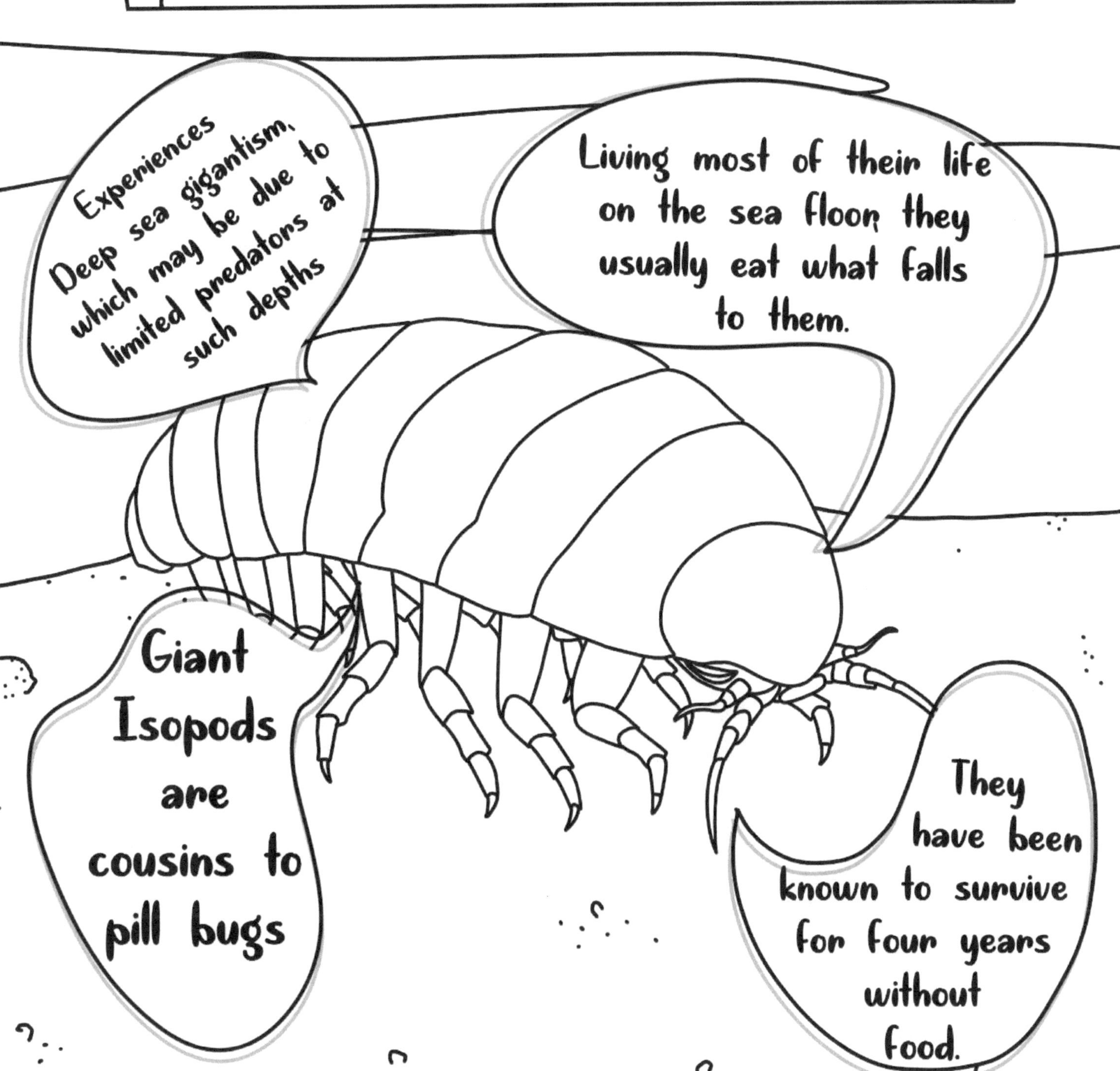
Experiences Deep sea gigantism, which may be due to limited predators at such depths
Living most of their life on the sea floor they usually eat what falls to them.
Giant Isopods are cousins to pill bugs
They have been known to survive for four years without food.

JAPANESE SPIDER CRAB

scientific name: Macrocheira kaempferi

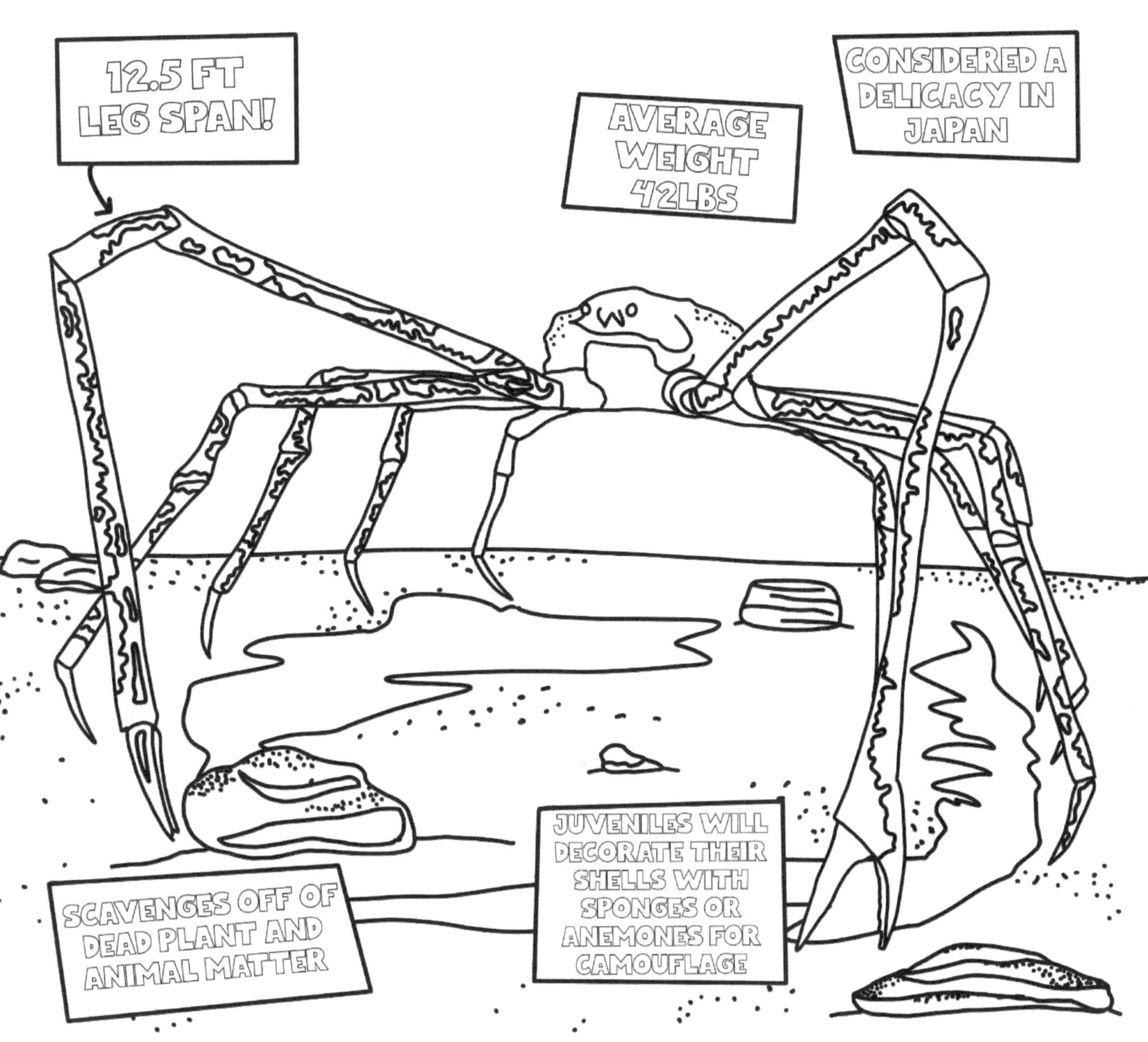
12.5 FT LEG SPAN!
AVERAGE WEIGHT 42LBS
CONSIDERED A DELICACY IN JAPAN
SCAVENGES OFF OF DEAD PLANT AND ANIMAL MATTER
JUVENILES WILL DECORATE THEIR SHELLS WITH SPONGES OR ANEMONES FOR CAMOUFLAGE

OPEN BRAIN CORAL

Scientific name: Trachyphyllia Geoffroyi

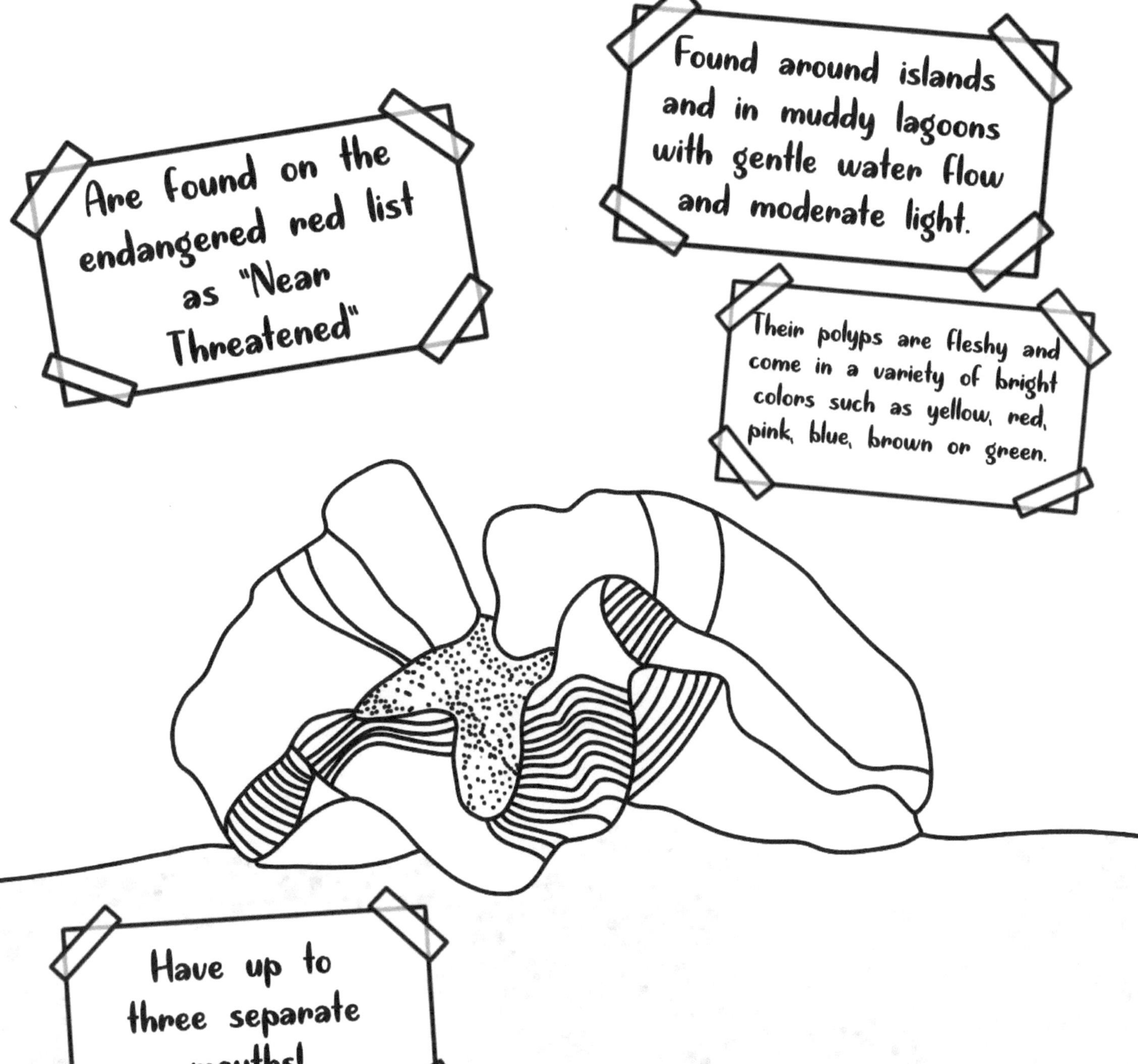
Are found on the endangered red list as "Near Threatened"
Found around islands and in muddy lagoons with gentle water flow and moderate light.
Their polyps are fleshy and come in a variety of bright colors such as yellow, red, pink, blue, brown or green.
Have up to three separate mouths!

PIRANHA
Inhabit murky, tropical waters
Bite with a maximum force of 72lbs. Their ancestors bit with a force of 1,068lbs.
Usually has 24 sharp teeth at any time
Spunky Science©

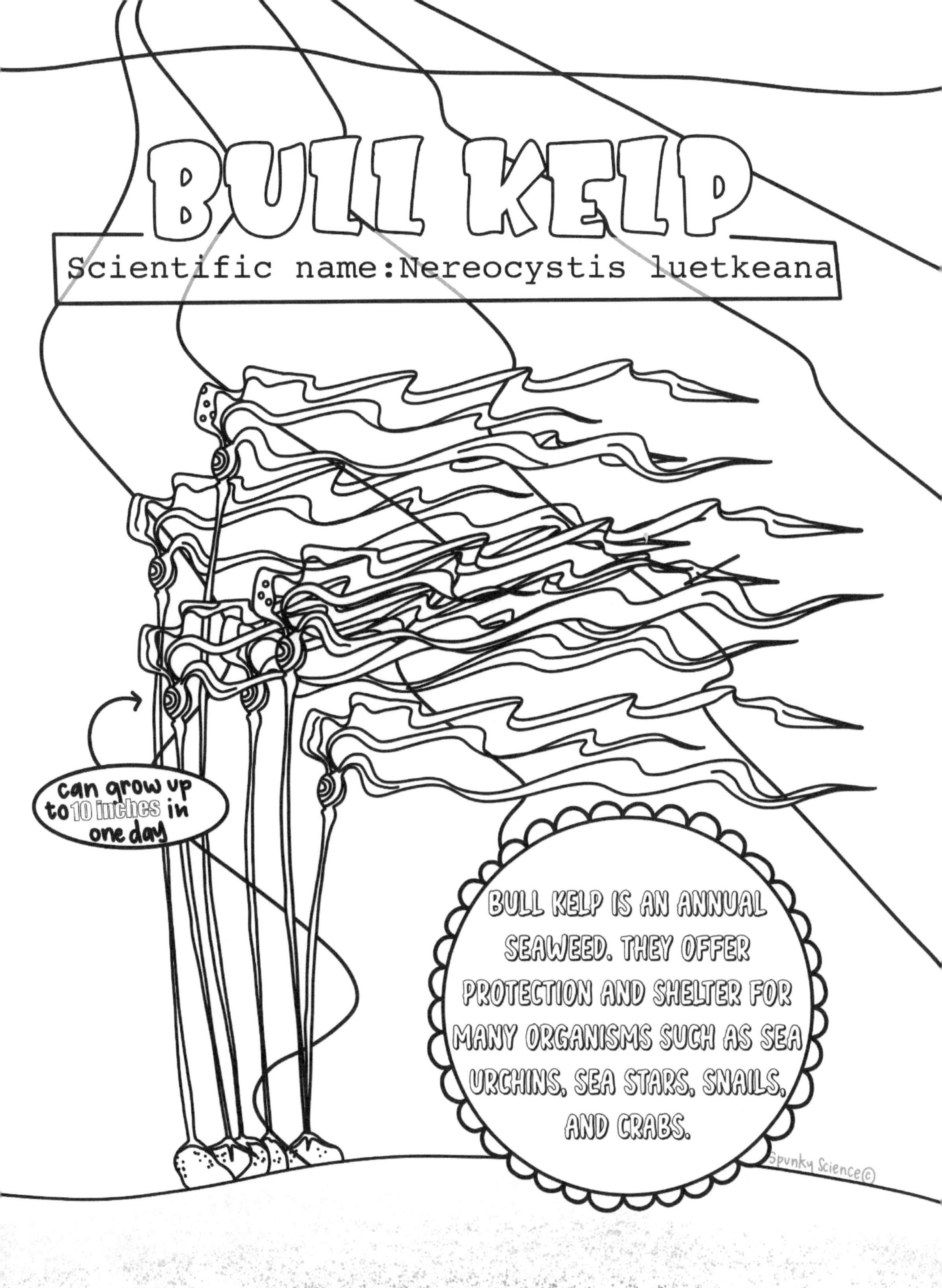
BULL KELP
Scientific name:Nereocystis luetkeana
can grow up to 10 inches in one day
BULL KELP IS AN ANNUAL SEAWEED. THEY OFFER PROTECTION AND SHELTER FOR MANY ORGANISMS SUCH AS SEA URCHINS, SEA STARS, SNAILS, AND CRABS.
Spunky Science©

GREEN SEA TURTLE

Scientific name: Chelonia mydas

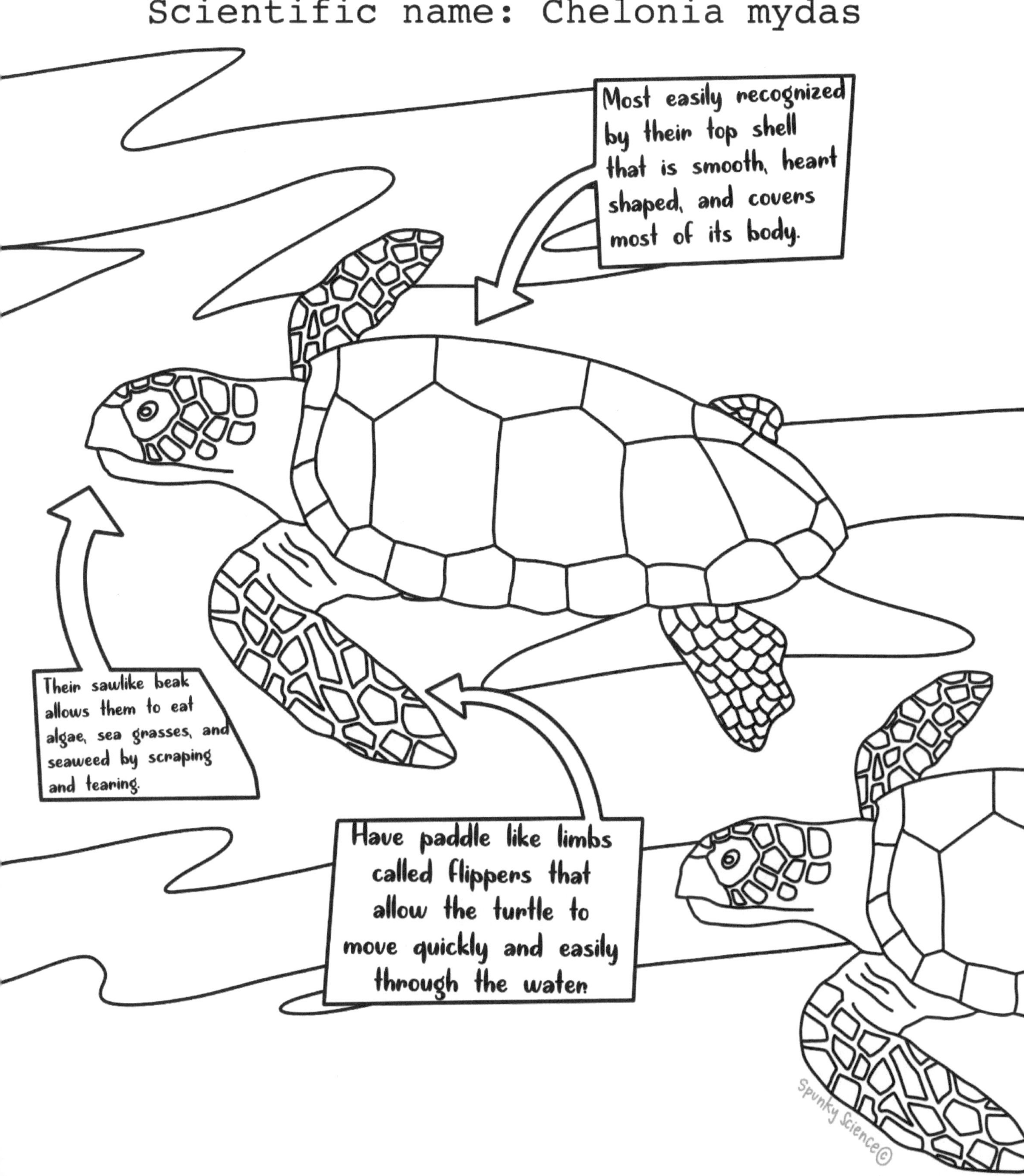
Most easily recognized by their top shell that is smooth, heart shaped, and covers most of its body.
Their sawlike beak allows them to eat algae, sea grasses, and seaweed by scraping and tearing.
Have paddle like limbs called flippers that allow the turtle to move quickly and easily through the water.
Spunky Science©

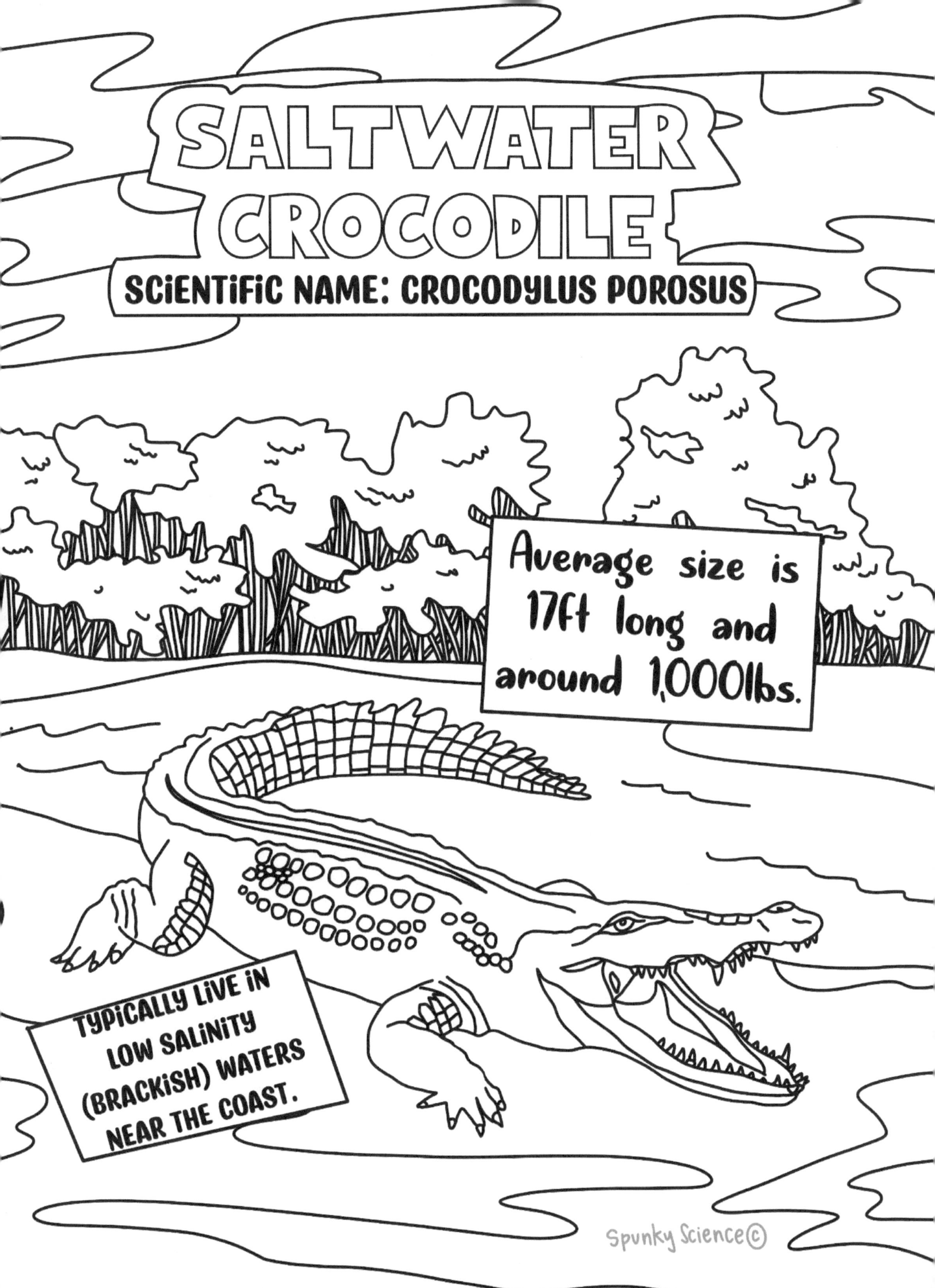
SALTWATER CROCODILE
SCIENTIFIC NAME: CROCODYLUS POROSUS
Average size is 17ft long and around 1,000lbs.
TYPICALLY LIVE IN LOW SALINITY (BRACKISH) WATERS NEAR THE COAST.
Spunky Science©

Copperband Butterflyfish

SCIENTIFIC NAME: CHEMON ROSTRATUS

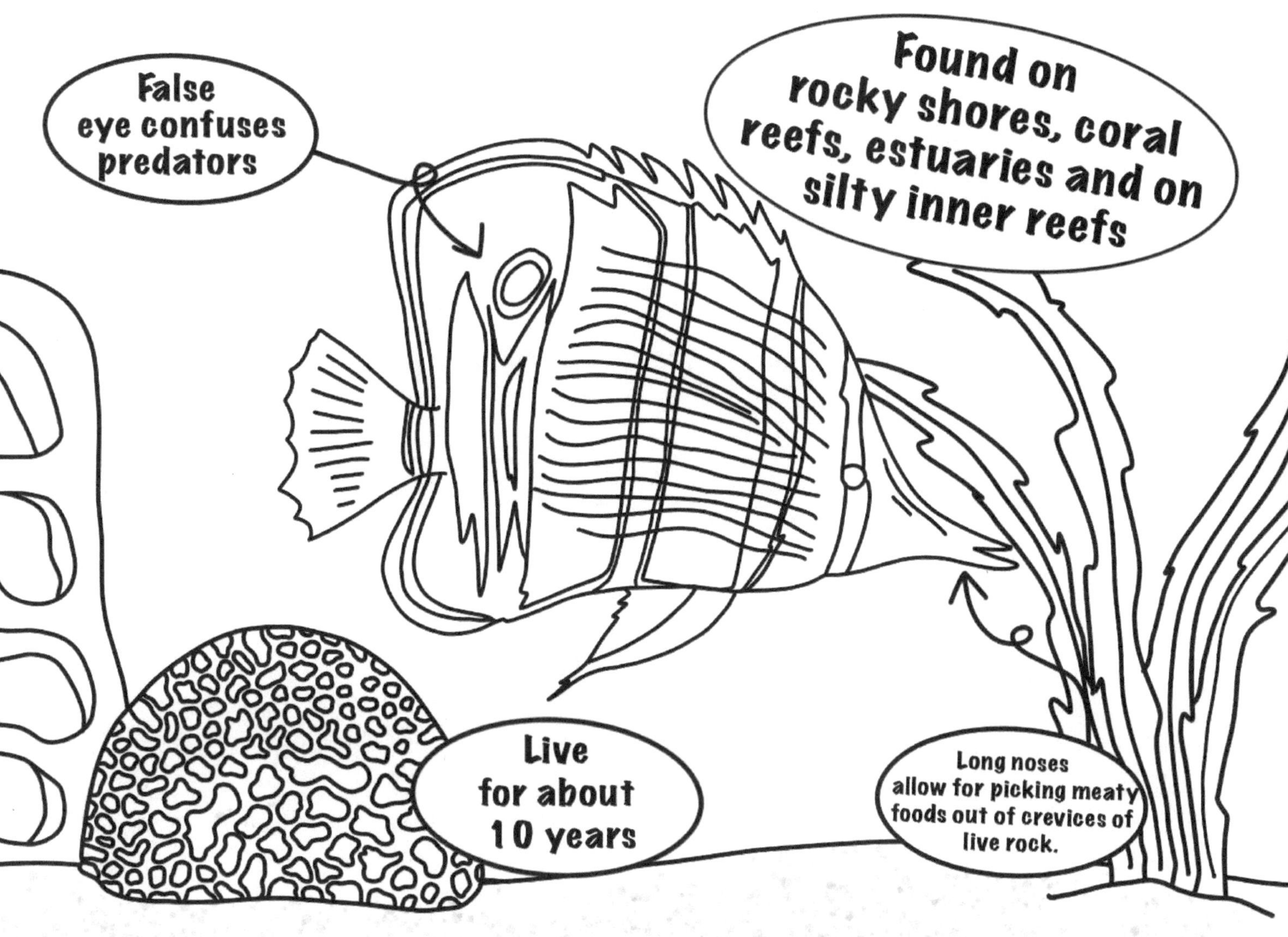
False eye confuses predators
Found on rocky shores, coral reefs, estuaries and on silty inner reefs
Live for about 10 years
Long noses allow for picking meaty foods out of crevices of live rock.

PEANUT WORM

Scientific name: Sipunculus nudus

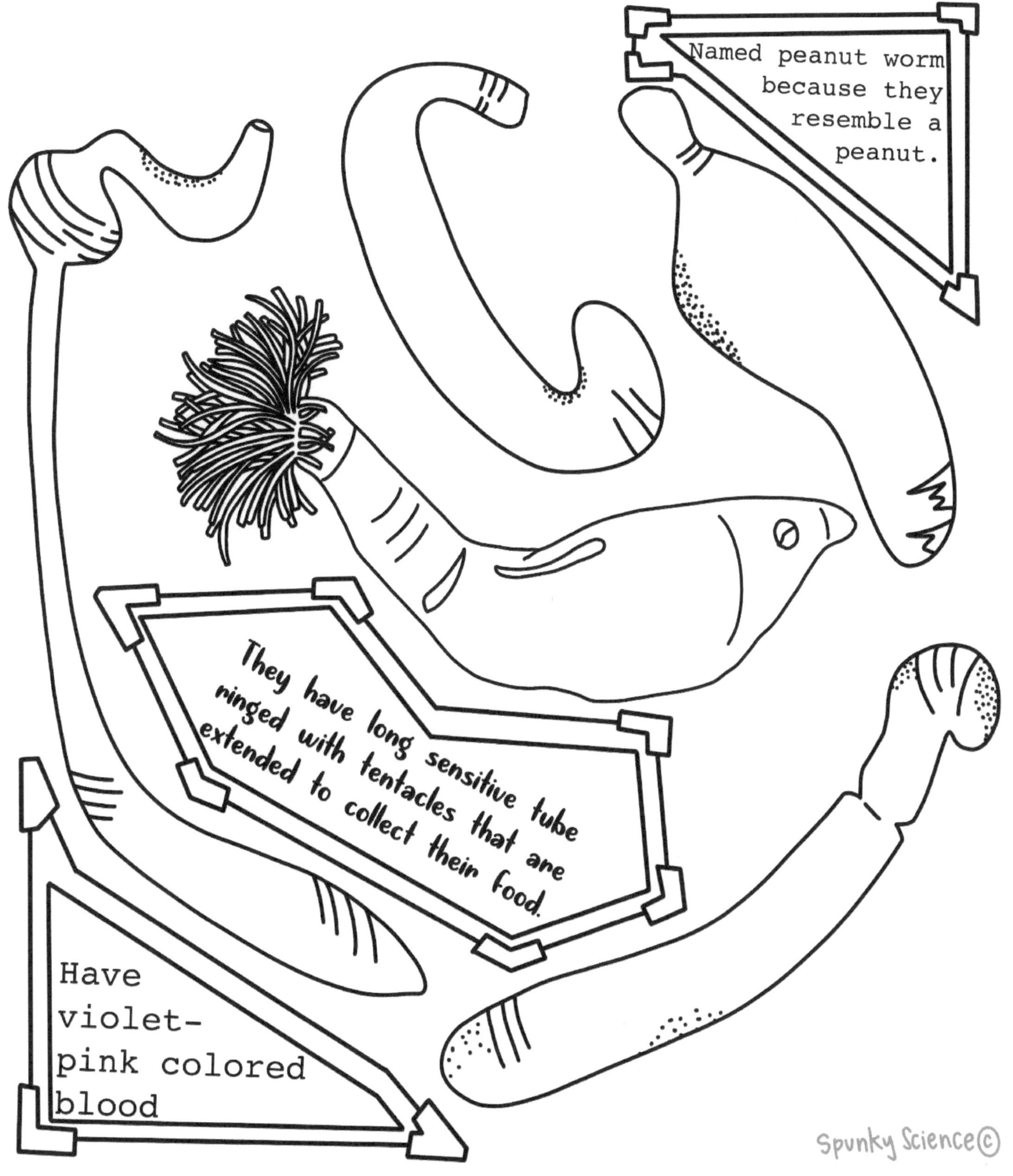

Named peanut worm because they resemble a peanut.
They have long sensitive tube ringed with tentacles that are extended to collect their food.
Have violet-pink colored blood

ANGLERFISH
Scientific name: Melanocetus johnsonii
The deep sea Anglerfish's lure is filled with bacteria that make their own light.
Due to their roundish shape and large heads, they aren't very good swimmers.
There are over 200 species of Anglerfish

MANDARINFISH

SCIENTIFIC NAME: SYNCHIROPUS SPLENDIDUS

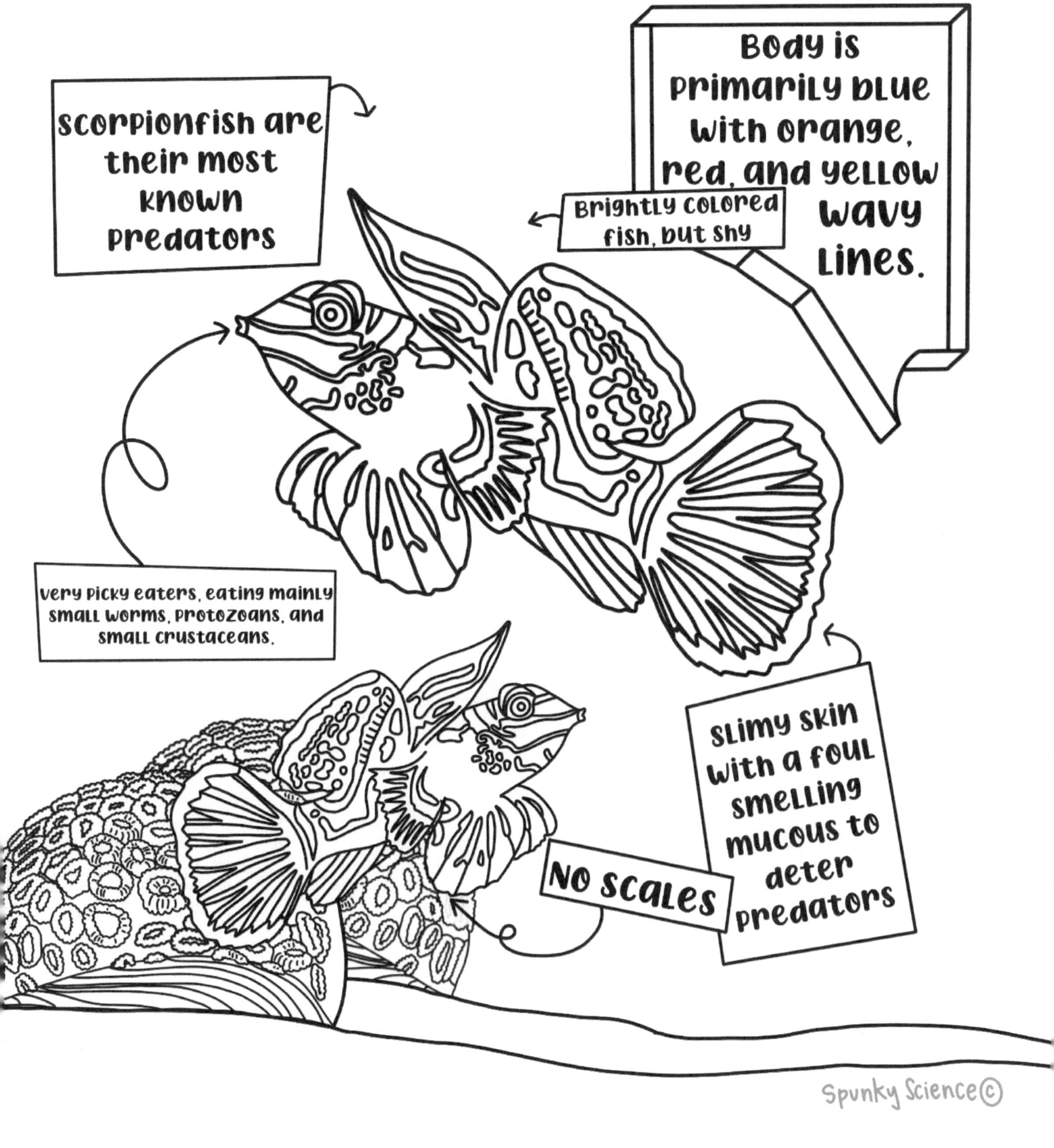

Body is primarily blue with orange, red, and yellow wavy lines.

Scorpionfish are their most known predators

Brightly colored fish, but shy

Very picky eaters, eating mainly small worms, protozoans, and small crustaceans.

Slimy skin with a foul smelling mucous to deter predators

No scales

WHALE SHARK

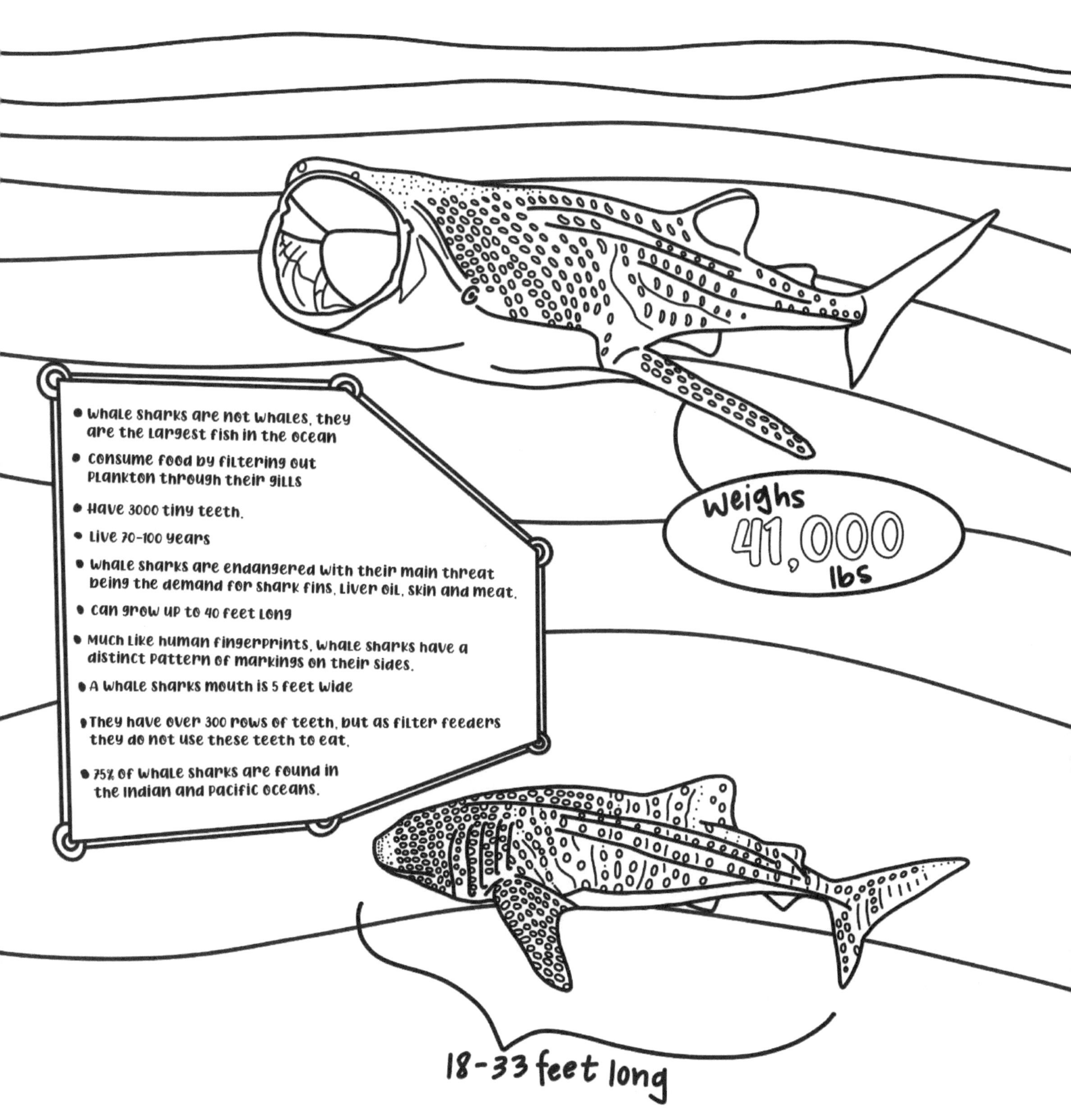

• Whale sharks are not whales, they are the largest fish in the ocean
• consume food by filtering out plankton through their gills
• Have 3000 tiny teeth.
• Live 70-100 years
• Whale sharks are endangered with their main threat being the demand for shark fins, liver oil, skin and meat.
• can grow up to 40 feet long
• Much like human fingerprints, whale sharks have a distinct pattern of markings on their sides.
• A whale sharks mouth is 5 feet wide
• They have over 300 rows of teeth, but as filter feeders they do not use these teeth to eat.
• 75% of whale sharks are found in the Indian and Pacific oceans.
weighs 41,000 lbs
18-33 feet long

HALFMOON BETTA FISH

Betta fish are native to Asia, where they live in the shallow water of marshes, ponds, or slow moving streams.

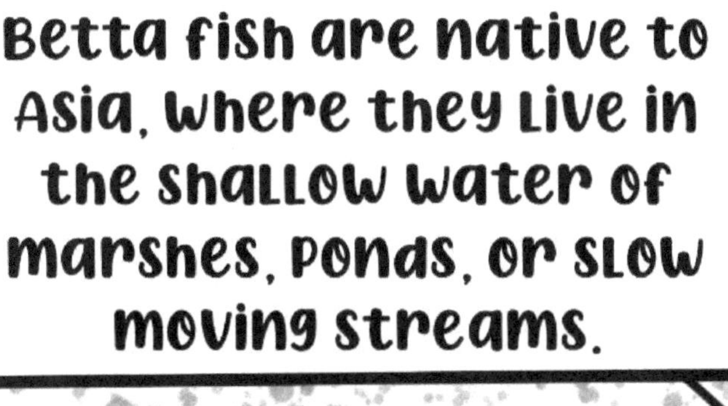

Their bright colors are from years of selective breeding. In the wild, Betta's are far less aggressive and have duller colors and smaller fins.

NECKLACE STARFISH

Scientific name: Fromia monilis

Lives in shallow water in a rocky environment.
Spines to protect from predators
Mouth
Feeds on encrusting sponges, detritus, small invertebrates

AFRICAN LUNGFISH

scientific name: protopterus annectens

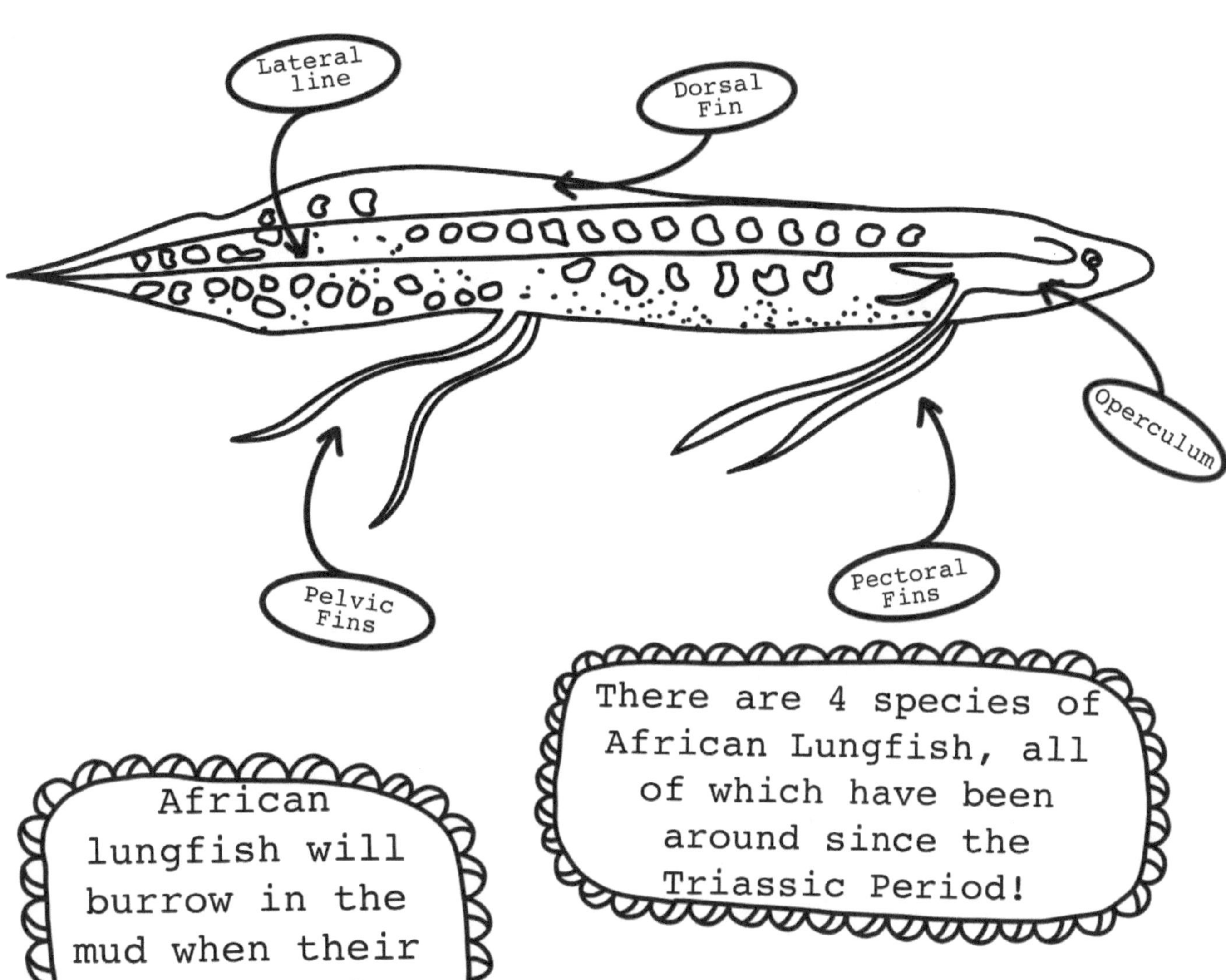
Lateral line
Dorsal Fin
Operculum
Pelvic Fins
Pectoral Fins
There are 4 species of African Lungfish, all of which have been around since the Triassic Period!
African lungfish will burrow in the mud when their water supply is diminished.

LEAFY SEADRAGON
Scientific name: Phycodurus eques

Leafy seadragon are not strong swimmers, so they rely heavily on their camouflage.

up to 30cm long

Eat plankton and small crustaceans

CLOWN FISH

SCIENTIFIC NAME: AMPHIPRION OCELLATIS

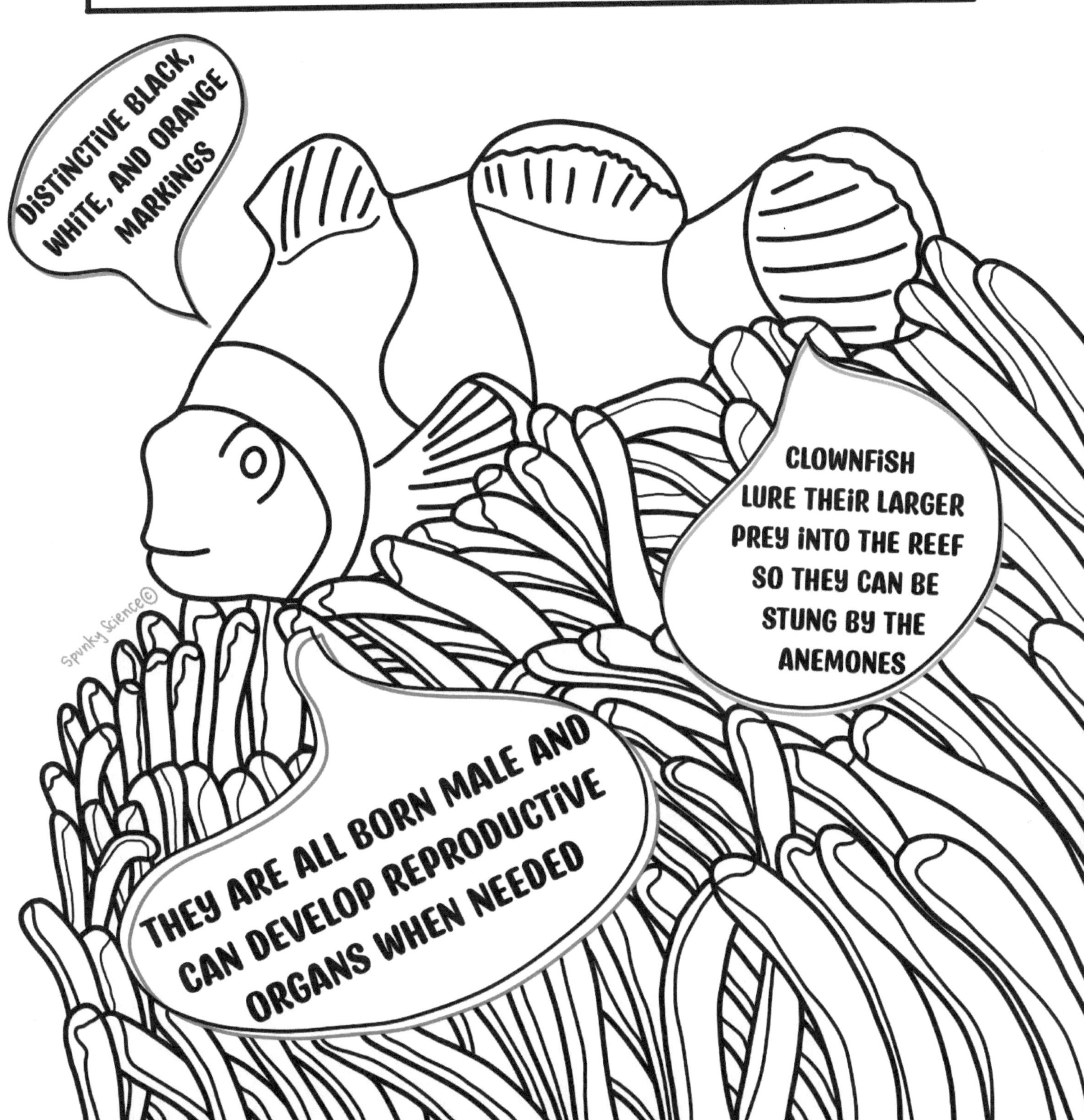

DISTINCTIVE BLACK, WHITE, AND ORANGE MARKINGS
CLOWNFISH LURE THEIR LARGER PREY INTO THE REEF SO THEY CAN BE STUNG BY THE ANEMONES
THEY ARE ALL BORN MALE AND CAN DEVELOP REPRODUCTIVE ORGANS WHEN NEEDED
Spunky Science©

STONEFISH

SCIENTIFIC NAME: SYNANCEIA VERRUCOSA

STONEFISH ARE THE MOST VENOMOUS FISH IN THE WORLD

USUALLY FOUND IN ROCKY REEFS NEAR THE COAST

EXCELLENT AT CAMOUFLAGE AND VERY FAST SWIMMERS

BASKING SHARK
Scientific name: Cetorhinus maximus

Not aggressive and are harmless to humans.

second Largest fish in the world 🌎

swim with their mouths open to filter the plankton out of the water for food.

Grow up to 45ft and 10,000lbs

CAULIFLOWER JELLYFISH

Scientific name: *Cephea cephea*

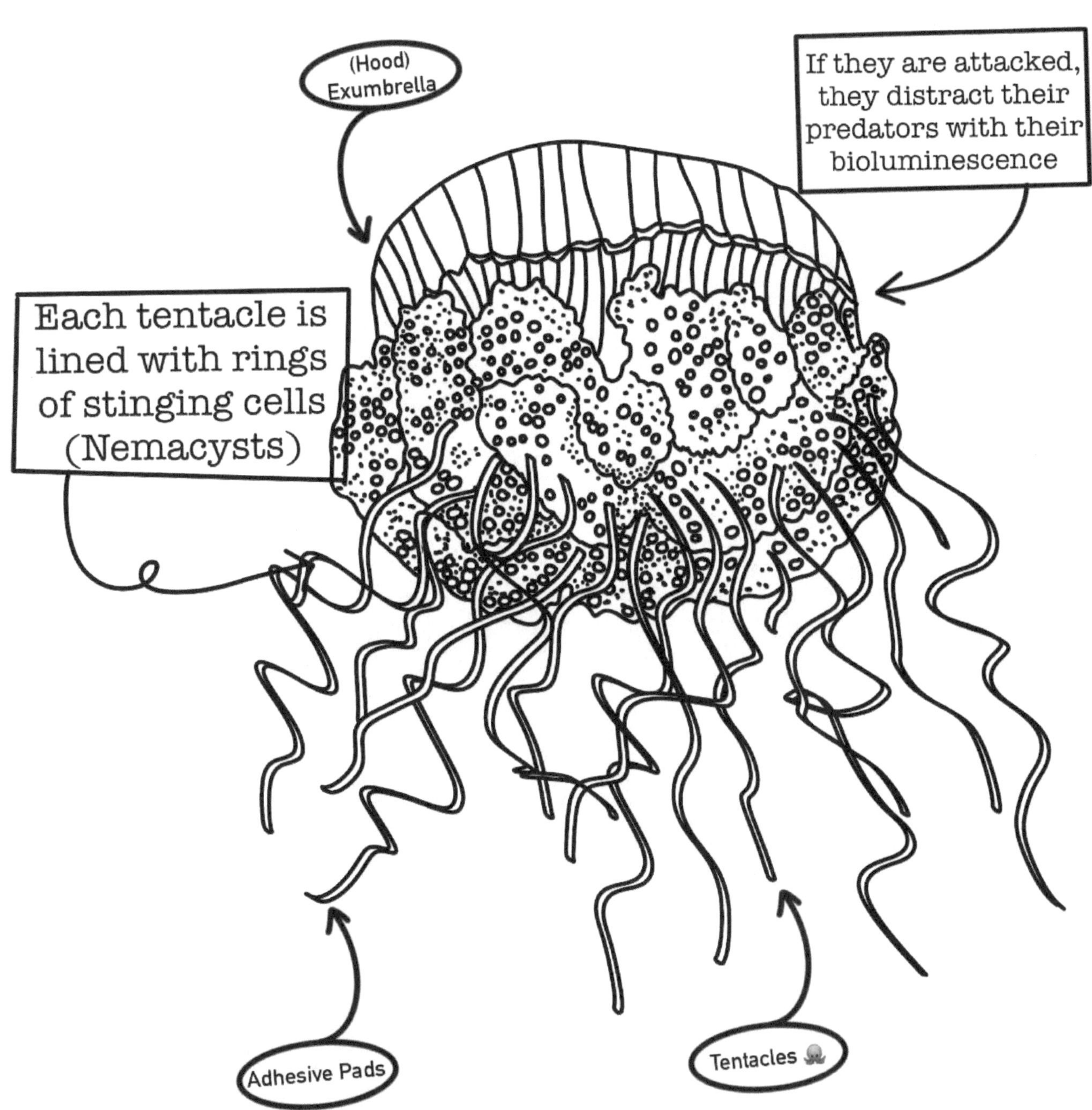
(Hood) Exumbrella
If they are attacked, they distract their predators with their bioluminescence
Each tentacle is lined with rings of stinging cells (Nemacysts)
Adhesive Pads
Tentacles

SAILFIN MOLLY
scientific name: Poecilia Latipinna
Spunky Science©
caudal fin
Dorsal fin
Mouth
5-3in in Length
pectoral fin
Prefer to Live in swamps, marshes, Lowland streams, and estuaries.
Characteristics:
Has an oblong body that is flat with an upturned mouth. Their caudal fin is Large and rounded as is their dorsal fin.

SPERM WHALE

SCIENTIFIC NAME: PHYSETER MACROCEPHALOUS

KNOWN FOR ITS HEAD BEING THE SIZE OF ABOUT ONE-THIRD OF ITS BODY SIZE

BREATHE THROUGH NOSTRILS CALLED A BLOWHOLE

THE CAUDAL FIN MOVES UP AND DOWN WITH POWERFUL MOVEMENTS CREATED BY POWERFUL MUSCLES ALONG THE PEDUNCLE.

Life expectancy: 70 yrs
Length: 52 feet
Mass: 30,000 to 90,000 pounds
Adaptation: Echolocation

SPERM WHALES HAVE THE LARGEST HEADS, THE BIGGEST BRAINS AND MAKE THE LOUDEST SOUND OF ANY ANIMAL ON EARTH!

GIANT PLUMOSE ANEMONE
scientific name: Metridium giganteum

Usually found attached to boats, rocks, or other hard surfaces

Diet consists of plankton and other microscopic organisms. To feed, they extend their tentacles and return it to their oral disc.

Usually eaten by the nudibranch

can reach 1 meter in height

GIANT SQUID

Scientific name: Architeuthis dux

A GIANT SQUID HAS 2 EYES, A BEAK, 8 ARMS, 2 FEEEDING TENTACLES, AND A SIPHON.

THEY USE THEIR FUNNEL TO PROPEL THEM BY SUCKING IN WATER AND THEN FORCING IT OUT BEHIND THEM.

AN EXAMPLE OF DEEP SEA GIGANTISM, GIANT SQUID GROW TO A SIZE OF 12-13 METERS

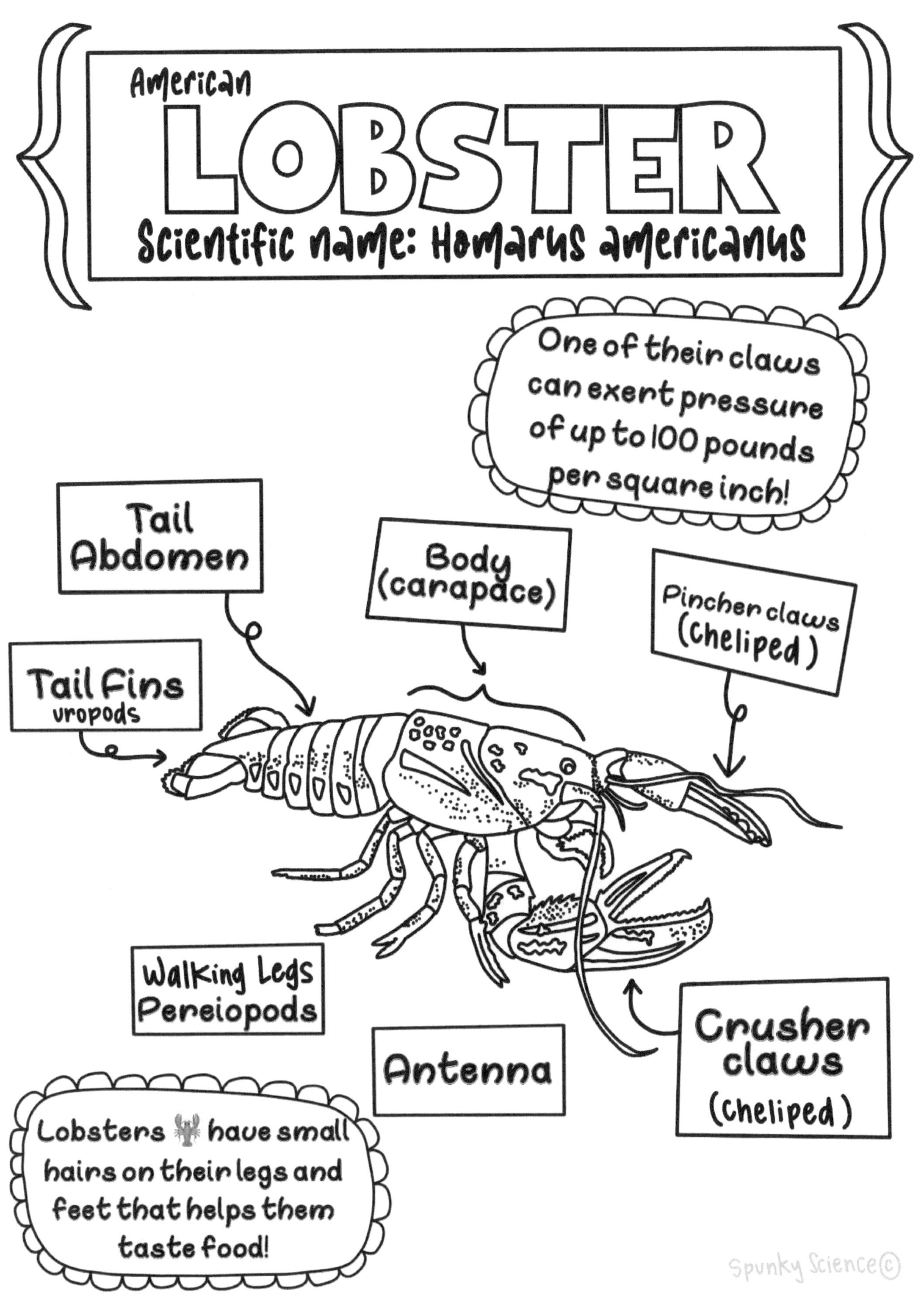
American
LOBSTER
Scientific name: Homarus americanus
One of their claws can exent pressure of up to 100 pounds per square inch!
Tail Abdomen
Body (carapace)
Pincher claws (Cheliped)
Tail Fins uropods
Walking Legs Pereiopods
Antenna
Crusher claws (Cheliped)
Lobsters have small hairs on their legs and feet that helps them taste food!

Made in United States
Troutdale, OR
02/16/2024